The
Philosophy
of the Christian
Curriculum

R.J. Rushdoony

CHALCEDON / ROSS HOUSE BOOKS
VALLECITO, CALIFORNIA

TABLE OF CONTENTS

Foreword. v

PART I

1 Religion, Culture & Curriculum 3
2 Changing a Curriculum. 13
3 Education & the Autonomy of Critical Thought. 15
4 The Curriculum & the Resurrection. 26

PART II

1 History Versus Social Science 37
2 Teaching Bible. 44
3 Grammar 48
4 Teaching Composition 51
5 Mathematics. 55
6 Teaching Civics, Government & Constitution. 59
7 Science 63
8 Science & Freedom 67
9 Teaching Science 71
10 The Experimental Method. 75
11 Music 79
12 Foreign Languages. 83

PART III

1 Education & the Fall: Up or Down?. 89
2 The Covenant: With God or Man? 95
3 Education & the Death of Man 99
4 Conflict & Resistance. 103
5 The Sovereignty of God in Education 108
6 Christian Education & the University. 114

PART IV

1 The Philosophy of Discipline 119
2 Student Problems 122
3 Humanism in the Classroom 126
4 The Teacher as Student 130
5 Sexual Differences in the Christian School 134
6 Whose Child?. 138
7 Biblical Motivation for Teachers and Students. 142
8 The Purpose of Learning 147
9 Education for Freedom 151
10 Education & Power 156
11 Theology & Pedagogy. 160
12 The Impossibility of Neutrality 164

PART V

1 Christianity Versus Humanism 171
2 Humanism: The Established Religion of State School 175
3 The Religious Goals of Humanism 184

General Index 191
Scripture Index. 201
Works Cited Index 203

FOREWORD

THE CHAPTERS OF this book were delivered as one or more lectures to a variety of groups. These include the Christian schools of Ohio conferences; Pensacola Christian College summer session (eighteen lectures); Via Vera Christian School in North Hollywood, California; the Alabama Christian Schools conventions; the Southern Association of Christian Schools; Christian Educators Association of the Southeast conventions; Fairfax Christian School; Trinity Christian School of Mesa, Arizona; the Michigan Association of Christian Schools; and the Church and School of Christian Liberty, Brookfield, Wisconsin.

The contents were written over a period of fifteen years, and sometimes expanded as Christian school teachers and administrators by the hundreds discussed these matters with me in question and answer sessions. This work was also submitted to the Valley Christian University, a graduate school in Clovis, California, as a part of their doctoral program and requirement.

I am deeply grateful to the many, many dedicated Christian school teachers and administrators who are the pioneers in the key area for our Christian future. I believe that their work is of unequalled importance in our history. I believe that the Christian schools will triumph and will educate all America in terms of God's Word and requirement. I believe that we shall see a steady stepping-up of the teaching, so that, in due time, the content will be increased, and the time span of education shortened. I believe that, in due time, the Christian school will teach *more* than is now taught in kindergarten through high school in seven or at most nine grades, so that students will enter colleges, universities, and vocational schools in their very early teens, and enter the world of work by the time that they are twenty. The Christian school movement is the Quiet Revolution of our time, and the great and enduring one.

I am grateful that I have had my small part in that revolution.

Rousas John Rushdoony
Chalcedon
Vallecito, California

Part I

Chapter 1

RELIGION, CULTURE & CURRICULUM

THE DICTIONARY DEFINITION of education describes it as "the impartation or acquisition of knowledge, skill, or discipline of character." The function of education is thus to school persons in the ultimate values of a culture. This is inescapably a *religious* task. Education has always been a religious function of society and closely linked to its religion. When a state takes over the responsibilities for education from the church or from Christian parents, the state has not thereby disowned all religions but simply disestablished Christianity in favor of its own statist religion, usually a form of humanism. An excellent means of analyzing the religion of any culture is to study its concept of education.

To see education as an expression of religion is not an approach limited to orthodox Christians. Liberals, anthropologists, and statist educators have so viewed it. According to a Columbia Teachers College publication, which defines religion, after Tillich, as "ultimate concern," religion is the framework of education:

> Religion as ultimate concern therefore provides the large framework within which education occurs. It determines perspective and basic orientation. It governs emphasis and fixes trends. Religious concern (whether or not recognized and designated as such) is the motive which actuates the educator and produces the general pattern of his work. The relationship between education and religion as ultimate concern is, in fact, a reciprocal one. Not only does religion provide the ultimate foundation for education, but education provides an admirable field for implementing religious commitments, thus making faith explicit in concrete act. A significant test of the governing religious convictions of a person or group is the character of the education promoted by that person or group.[1]

1. Philip H. Phenix, *Religious Concerns in Contemporary Education* (New York, NY:

Not only does education find its foundation in religion, but the educational *curriculum* expresses the religious standards and expectations of a culture. The Latin word "curriculum," from which the English word is taken without change of spelling, means a running, a race course, chariot, and is cognate with the Latin verb, *currere*, to run. A curriculum is thus the chariot, race course, or vehicle whereby a culture expresses its religious faith and standards. The basic curriculum is called the liberal arts curriculum, "liberal" from the Latin *liber*, free, and it is a course in the *arts of freedom*, or a vehicle in *the arts of liberty*. A liberal arts curriculum is thus a practical answer to the question, *What is liberty?* And, *How does a man prepare himself to be a free man?*

The modern liberal arts curriculum is the long development of a humanistic religious answer to this question. Hellenic in origin, it gives us a man-centered and essentially anti-Christian answer to the question, *How shall a man be free?* This question is basically the same as the one asked within the sphere of religion: *How shall a man be saved?* The liberal arts curriculum is thus the channel of liberty and of salvation. It is the means whereby a culture saves its children from the encroaching evils and threats, and prepares them for life in terms of the knowledge, skill, or discipline of character required to be a free man. And this is inescapably a religious task.

The origin of the modern curriculum is in Greek humanism, and it should be noted that Greek culture was humanistic, but not individualistic. Werner Jaeger has noted that, "The intellectual principle of the Greeks is not individualism but 'humanism,' to use the word in its original and classical sense...It meant the process of educating man into his true form, the real and genuine human nature."[2] Bowra has also cited this humanistic orientation:

Because they believed in their own human nature and liked to see it harmoniously at work, the Greeks developed a morality which was founded on human nature and able to operate freely and confidently without worrying too much what the gods thought about it.[3]

Bureau of Publications, Teachers College, Columbia University, 1959), p. 19.

2. Werner Jaeger, *Paideia: The Ideals of Greek Culture*, vol. 1, trans. from the 2nd German edition, Gilbert Highet, ed. (New York, NY: Oxford, 1945), p. xxiii.

3. C. M. Bowra, *The Greek Experience* (Cleveland, OH: The World Publishing Co.,

Greek education reflected this humanistic faith. Poetry held a place of importance comparable to the Bible, except that no written work had any binding power. Homer, however, had a religious significance, in that he wrote of *heroes*, the real gods of Greece.

The dance and the gymnasium were important, not for physical exercise, but for religious reasons. Enthusiastic dancing had as its goal being god-possessed and god-filled, incarnating the divinity which was potentially realizable by all men. Physical development had, not mere health as its goal, but the realization of the *idea* of man, a divine humanity, the perfection of form. The goal of man was to be an incarnation of the idea, the universal, and hence the study of geometry, of abstract forms, was more religious than practical, or, more accurately, was practical because religious. The importance of geometry in the modern curriculum, and its priority over many studies much more relevant to the world around us, is an evidence of the continuing hold of the Greek curriculum on us. The modern physical education class is, in terms of its professed purpose, an anomaly. Ostensibly, the school wants to give the child an opportunity for physical exercise. It therefore provides bus transportation to and from school and prevents children from exercising themselves by walking a mile or two! The purpose of physical education classes is not exercise but planned recreation, group activity, and, very definitely in many cases, games and dances deemed psychologically advantageous to "liberal" education. Greek education was also geared to the *polis*, the city-state. Man, for Aristotle, was a political animal, and hence man was to be educated into the saving life of the state. Plato's *Republic* was a plan for total education for total statism.

This statist purpose of humanistic education was even more clearly emphasized by the Romans. According to Grimal, "Roman morality has a very distinct aim — the subordination of the individual to the City."[4] Religion and piety had reference to the city, for the gods were the gods of the city, and religion, by binding men to the gods, bound them to the city of the gods. According to Barrow,

---

1957), p. 55.

4. Pierre Grimal, *The Civilization of Rome*, W. S. Maguinness, trans. (New York, NY: Simon and Schuster, 1963), p. 100.

For a "religious man" the phrase is usually "a man of the highest *pietas*," and *pietas* is part of that subordination of which we have spoken. You are *pius* to the gods if you admit their claims: you are *pius* to your parents and elders, and children and friends, and country and benefactors, and all that excites, or should excite, your regard and perhaps your affection, if you admit their claims on you, and discharge your duty accordingly; the claims exist because the relationships are sacred.[5]

The liberal arts curriculum thus had a statist orientation. Man's liberty, man's salvation, was to be found in faithful subordination of himself and all his being to the City of Man. The chief end of man, a political and social animal, was to glorify the state and to serve and enjoy it all the days of his life.

It is not surprising, therefore, that Christianity came into rapid conflict with Rome and the entire world. It was a battle between Christ and Caesar, between the City of God and the City of Man, for the control of the world and of history. On the one hand, the emphasis was on the triune God and on His eternal decree, on the primacy of eternity; and on the other hand, the emphasis was on the primacy of time, on the civil order as the order of incarnation and divinity, and on the temporal decree of the total state.

A Christian order did emerge in measure, and education began to turn increasingly to the Bible for its norms, but the prevalence of Platonistic and Neoplatonistic strains, as evidenced in such conservatives as Hugh of St. Victor,[6] and the rise of Aristotelianism, steadily undermined the theocentric emphasis. Gradually, the basic Greco-Roman humanism gained ascendency, and the City of Man became united to the City of God in name, and the Church of Rome became this true state. True education and piety involved submission to Rome. Education had, as an addition to it, celibacy as a requirement, total dedication to this very present city, the Church of Rome. Bishop Otto of Freising sorrowfully noted that, "I seem to myself to have composed a history not of two cities but virtually of one only, which I call the Church."[7] The true *polis* or City of Man was

---

5. R. H. Barrow, *The Romans* (Chicago, IL: Aldine Publishing Co., [1949] 1964), p. 22.

6. See Jerome Taylor, ed., *The Didascalion of Hugh of St. Victor* (New York, NY: Columbus, 1961).

7. Otto, Bishop of Freising, *The Two Cities: A Chronicle of Universal History to the Year*

now the church, the voice and champion of the reviving humanism. The very deeply rooted Christian nature of what is called "medieval" Europe must not be underrated or overlooked, but the Greco-Roman humanism steadily regained ground and conquered the intellectuals of Christendom and triumphed in education. The curriculum was simply an adaptation of ancient humanism.

The Renaissance accentuated this rebellion against Christianity and was a logical development of the long tradition of man-centered educational theory. Instead, however, of emphasizing the church as the true *polis* or state, the Renaissance emphasized the amoral power-state and individual, anarchistic man. God and law had dropped out of the picture, and both man and the state faced the world uninhibited by the restrictions of Christian faith and morality. According to White, in the Renaissance, in the state this meant *tyranny*, and in the personal realm, *anarchy*:

> The Prince rules according to the motto, "First my will, then the right." *"Tel est notre bon plaisir."* The action of the social nihilist stands under the aegis: "Break the chains which hamper your personal liberty." In both, an energetic activistic component is manifest.[8]

This coincidence of anarchism and tyranny is not accidental. Both are the products of nihilism, relativism, and pragmatism. When God is man's universal, man is dependent upon God as the focus of his life, and the source of his law, standard, status, and salvation. Man can then be independent of man because he is dependent upon God. He acts and performs his calling with reference to the eyes of God primarily, rather than the eyes of man. The humanist, however, has only man as his audience. In every man-centered faith, "the individual needs society as a resonance box."[9] *For humanism, man is his own law and his own lawmaker, so that social approval is the best test of law.* This standard leads inevitably to the socialization of life, law, and living, because man must move in terms of man as his god and law. Instead of declaring God to be the universal,

---

1146 A.D., ed. and trans. C. C. Mierow, A. P. Evans, C. Knapp (New York, NY: Columbia University Press, 1928), p. 323.

8. John S. White, *Renaissance Cavalier* (New York, NY: Philosophical Library, 1959), p. 7.

9. ibid., p. 8.

man becomes the universal and the source of meaning and being. "The medieval saint was virtuous in the desert also. The invisible eyes of God hovered above him. Universal Man needs society in order to display his virtues. His realm is only of this world."[10] Thus, wherever education becomes humanistic, it will produce both statism and anarchistic individualism. Man's only law will become himself and other men. Moreover, a curriculum which professes to be Christian because it includes religious instruction but is in all else humanistic in orientation will also breed statism and anarchism. The center of the stage becomes man without law, i.e., without God's law, and the amoral state and amoral anarchistic man then predominate.

The Reformation emphasized the sovereignty of God and the total scope of His law, i.e., predestination. Humanism was thus in principle denied. The function of education and of the curriculum was the preparation of man to glorify God, to enjoy Him, and to serve Him in and through a chosen calling. In the United States, the Christian school developed to a degree unknown in Europe, where the humanistic past and the Enlightenment hindered the development of a Christian curriculum. Until Horace Mann, all American education was Christian. The educational accomplishments of America were without equal in the world, as noted in a report in 1800 by a Frenchman, Du Pont de Nemours, *National Education in the United States of America*. The result practically was a high literacy rate, with illiteracy almost nonexistent, and only four in a thousand being unable to write legibly and neatly, according to this report, with excellent abilities in the basic skills manifested by virtually all. The religious instruction was also excellent. In 1815, the average age of criminals in the United States was forty-five, in 1960, nineteen. Because men were taught to be dependent upon God, they were independent of man and the state. Their source of security was neither the anarchistic individual nor the amoral state, but the sovereign and triune God.

The Enlightenment came as a countermovement to the Reformation and a revival of the ancient Greco-Roman humanism. Its philosophical premise was the dialectic of *nature* and *liberty*. *Nature* was introduced as

---

10. ibid., pp. 8–9.

a substitute concept for God, and natural law, which meant whatever the philosophers chose to call it, took the place of the hard and fast written Word of God. After Darwin, *nature* became an invalid concept; "nature" is blindly evolving and is without mind or reason. If there is to be law, then it must be man's law, so that statism succeeded the older liberalism of natural law as the new source of authority and law. But law is in this new sense *anti*-law, i.e., a denial that there is any absolute law in the universe, any truth beyond pragmatic truth. As a result, the whole curriculum becomes progressive, i.e., instrumental. No subject embodies any truth; all ideas are tools for man's use in self-realization. *Liberty* therefore means *freedom from law* as absolute, law as embodying truth and moral order. If truth be denied, then equality is possible, because all ideas are equally valid and equally false; their status is in utility, instrumentality, and nothing more. For the curriculum, this means "teaching children, not subject matter," and teaching children means teaching them this total relativism, so that *no truth* exists except man, and man realizes himself in and through the Great Society of Dewey and others, the total state. Thus, for Dewey, orthodox Christianity, with its belief in truth and error, good and evil, heaven and hell, the saved and the lost, is antidemocratic and irreconcilable with a democratic society.[11] *Biblical Christianity* thus has no place in the curriculum and therefore in the life of the Great Society. But, according to Conant, the *family* is an aristocratic institution also, and one that ensures that "inequality of opportunity is automatically, and often unconsciously, a basic principle of the nation." To hold democracy and equality and maintain a family-based society is to create "a perpetual compromise."[12] Thus, the family has no place in the curriculum in any Christian sense and is rapidly being crowded out in life.

The basic premise of the state school's curriculum is humanism, *relativistic* humanism. The liberal arts, the arts of freedom, involve the abandonment of God, truth, and law for the affirmation of man. This is an unconditional affirmation: all things are relative to man and have a pragmatic truth in relationship to him.

---

11. John Dewey, *A Common Faith* (New York, NY: Yale University Press, 1934), p. 84.

12. James Bryant Conant, *Education in a Divided World: The Function of the Public School in Our Unique Society* (Cambridge, MA: Harvard University Press, 1948), p. 8.

A Christian curriculum must be developed, therefore. The centrality of Biblical instruction is basic to the liberal arts of Christian education. But the rest of the curriculum must be revised in terms of Christian liberty, the arts of Christian freedom and dominion under God. The study of *law* is therefore necessary. We live in a world governed by law, and yet our modern curriculum still reflects the Greek curriculum's disinterest in law. The Roman approach treated law as a product of the state, and the highest law was the health or welfare of the people. True law was thus relative to man, pragmatic, and hence subordinate to the state. Thus, any reference to law, and obedience to law, was a branch of political studies, of *civics* or of *government*, because the state was above the law. In the modern curriculum, neither in grade school, high school, nor college, is a general course in law taught, except for business law courses, and references to law in civics and government courses. But, for the Christian, law is not under the state or a product of the state, but an expression of God's holiness and order. The state is subordinate to law, and the meaning of law must be central. And a man is not truly educated in our modern world if he is ignorant of the nature and meaning of law. Many states require a course in the U.S. Constitution; the Christian school should also require a course in the nature and meaning of law.

Another area of importance: one of the major problems confronting man is his relationship to his environment, the world he is born into and the world he reacts to and in part remakes. Ecology, although very often fallacious from a Christian perspective, is thus a very important area of study. Man cannot usurp the role of God in his relationship to the world, but neither can he treat himself as a creature of his environment, since he is created in God's image. The study of ecology is thus of major importance to Christian liberal arts.

The approach to history in a Christian curriculum is of necessity radically different. From the perspective of humanism, the determination of history is from within time and, potentially at least, by man. From the Biblical perspective, time and history are alike determined from all eternity by the triune God. Thus, the philosophy of history varies. The subject matter does also. The term "Middle Ages" is revelatory of the bias of modern historiography. It views real history, significant history, as ancient

Greco-Roman humanism, followed by the "darkness" of a Christian era, and then finally reborn with the Renaissance. The "Middle Ages" were thus a kind of historical recess, lapse, or blank spot. The "Dark Ages" were not dark but alive with new impetus and a new inventiveness.[13] The "Middle Ages" cannot be read in terms of the post-Trentine church, nor in terms of the centrality of the papacy.

Economics deserves a place in the high school curriculum, not as a branch of civics or civil government, but as an independent law sphere. Literature needs a reevaluation of its position. The modern thesis of Shelley, that poets are the uncrowned legislators of the world, rests on the ancient and pagan concept of the inspired bard, who incarnates in himself the divinity of being. Instead of a humanistic perspective, a Christian perspective must prevail. The neglect of such literary gems as the sonnets of David Gray, and the poems of Fulke Greville, needs to be remedied. Psychology has, in the modern curriculum, taken the place of theology as the guide to life. Anthropology also increasingly speaks with authority concerning man's life. But anthropology, the doctrine of man, and psychology, the doctrine of the soul, were once aspects of theology, and in a Christian curriculum must be restored to theology.

In approaching the *sciences*, it must be denied that such a thing as *science* exists. No workable definition of "science" is possible. If it be defined as a body of organized knowledge, the term can be applied to virtually every field. If it be defined as experimentally verifiable knowledge, then astronomy is excluded, as well as geology and other studies. Just as there exists no religion in general, but many particular religions, so no science in general can be defined, but only particular sciences. Moreover, in approaching any particular science and any body of scientific thought, we must deny that we are confronted merely with a body of facts. The facts are set in the context of interpretations, and interpretations rest on pretheoretical religious presuppositions, as Cornelius Van Til and Herman Dooyeweerd have pointed out. To accept the universe as ultimate and self-created is a great act of faith, but it is a non-Christian faith. To assume the ultimacy of chance as against the ultimacy of God and His eternal decree

13. See William Carroll Bark, *Origins of the Medieval World* (Palo Alto, CA: Stanford University Press, 1958).

is equally an act of faith. Both the Christian and the humanist begin with an act of faith, but the humanist strives to persuade the Christian that this difference between them is one of faith versus knowledge, when it is a clash of faiths in which we must hold that truth and knowledge are with Christian faith.

A great evil introduced into Christianity, Pietism, led to a surrender of knowledge and the world to the unbeliever and a withdrawal of the Christian to a purely inner world of experience. As a result, relevance to the world and to knowledge came to mean secularism, and the church moved from a theocentric orientation to a man-centered and experiential emphasis. The result was a surrender of the world and of education to humanism. Only by reclaiming the entire curriculum as the curriculum of Christian liberty, as the Christian liberal arts course, can education be again a liberating force, and man be delivered from the devastating and enslaving forces of amoral statism and anarchistic individualism. A Christian curriculum is thus a major and urgent necessity.

A state curriculum, to be true to itself, must teach statism. A Christian curriculum, to be true to itself, must be in every respect Christian.

Chapter 2

CHANGING A CURRICULUM

BASIC TO A sound educational enterprise is a changing curriculum. Precisely because a sound curriculum has as its foundation an unchanging faith in the sovereign and triune God and His infallible Word, it will therefore recognize that man and his problems will change and develop. The area of the unchanging is in God and eternity, not in time and man. When China adopted a relativistic faith in change as ultimate, its education became static and unchanging, because no transcendental God and law remained to provide a critique of history or a principle of differentiation. Without an absolute law, all things are relative and equal, equally important and at the same time equally meaningless. At the moment, one option may seem better than another, but who is to judge that the moment has any meaning, or that options are anything but illusions?

The static nature of the curriculum is apparent in language studies, which are still geared to an absolute world. Latin was once the language of scholarship and an international language; its only value now is to historians and classical scholarship. Greek and Hebrew are important to a Christian society, but basically only to the Biblical scholarship of that society. German and to a degree French are of value to potential historians, and to the limited few who travel extensively, but to few others. The influence of politics has led to some stress on Russian and Chinese, but a wiser, economic perspective would stress Japanese, for Japan is today the world's second greatest industrial power. The potential development of Brazil might be important to curriculum makers and merits consideration. Briefly, foreign studies need to be geared to reality, not the past.

Similarly, in mathematics, much of the curriculum is important to future mathematicians, not to the overwhelming majority of peoples.

Mathematics should be geared more to management, accounting, and a variety of practical needs of the modern world. Such a revision of the curriculum would actually require upgrading the content of the mathematics curriculum rather than a cheapening of it.

In literature, not the craft of the writer but the expressions of ideas, faiths, and cultures merits serious attention and is most needed by the student.

The Bible and Biblical law are basic to any sound curriculum and cannot be excluded without inviting educational anarchy.

Economics is a basic requirement of every sound curriculum and should be a thorough analysis of theory and practice.

The sound curriculum will be the relevant curriculum, and relevancy requires two factors, a world of absolutes, and a world of change. It is not enough to hold to God's absolutes: they must be continually and freshly related to the changing times.

Relevancy is more than subjects: it is also a faith which makes connections, establishes relationships, and grows by its ability to bring things into meaningful and useful relationships. This involves the personal element. A retarded fourth-grade boy, placed in Fairfax Christian School, Fairfax, Virginia, in the school year of 1969–1970, was later tested by psychologists and found to have an IQ of 76. Nonetheless, this boy, in a school of superior children, scored, on standard, national achievement tests at the end of the year, at grade or above grade at all points. Basic to this success was a sound curriculum and thoughtful Christian teachers. A curriculum cannot be relativistic without failure, but it must be relevant. In this case, both curriculum and teachers brought Christian relevance to the boy, with outstanding success.

Chapter 3

EDUCATION & THE AUTONOMY
OF CRITICAL THOUGHT

THE *philosophes* OF the Enlightenment attacked Christian faith and thought with unrelenting hostility and venom. As Peter Gay admitted, in Voltaire's case, that *philosophe* "publicly denounced the Jesuits as power-mad, sly, and as a lot, revolting pederasts," but "privately conceded that his old Jesuit teachers had been decent men and respectable scholars."[1] His language with reference to the clergy was consistently vicious and coarse; Voltaire spoke of them as, "those buggers, the Reverend Fathers,"[2] and used many other terms of abuse. It was, of course, Voltaire himself who was sexually derelict. As a young man, he had "coopted into a precious society of wealthy gourmands, brilliant talkers, and homosexuals, who took impiety for granted — it was the mark of membership."[3]

Voltaire's problem was that no term was for him sufficient to express the infamy of Christianity. The battle cry of Voltaire, and of the Enlightenment, *ecrasez l'infame*, was not merely directed against the church, but "was directed against Christianity itself, against Christian dogma in all its forms, Christian institutions, Christian ethics, and the Christian view of man."[4] Christianity had to be destroyed to remove from man the shame and disgrace which it conveyed.

The basic and central offense of Christianity was its doctrine of authority, the concept that an absolute and sovereign God has an absolute

---

1. Peter Gay, *The Enlightenment: An Interpretation, vol. 1: The Rise of Modern Paganism* (New York, NY: Alfred A. Knopf, 1967), p. 24.

2. ibid., p. 388.

3. ibid., p. 385.

4. ibid., p. 59.

authority over man, is man's only savior, and provides man with an infallible Word. As Peter Gay correctly insisted, "the citadel" of Greek thought, of Renaissance philosophy, and Enlightenment faith, was "the autonomy of critical thought."[5] Christian thought might well be highly intellectual, rational, empirical, or scientific, but, as long as it moved in terms of Christian faith, it was anathema. The Christian concept of authority was seen as the betrayal of man. The Biblical, the Augustinian concept, asserted the priority of faith. The prophet Isaiah had said, "If ye will not believe, surely ye shall not be established" (Isa. 7:9), translated by the Septuagint: unless you believe, you will not understand. Faith precedes knowledge, blessing, and works. St. Anselm summed up the Biblical position simply:

> I do not endeavor, O Lord, to penetrate thy sublimity, for in no wise do I compare my understanding with that; but I long to understand in some degree thy truth, which my heart believes and loves. For I do not seek to understand that I may believe, but I believe in order to understand. For this also I believe, — that unless I believed, I should not understand.[6]

Herman Dooyeweerd has amply demonstrated that all theoretical thought rests on basically and essentially religious presuppositions which provide the framework for theoretical thinking.[7] Theoretical thought is thus the product of pre-theoretical religious assumptions. The Enlightenment and modern faith in the autonomy of theoretical thought is neither a rational nor an empirical conclusion, nor a scientific report: it is a religious faith and presupposition.

But the faith of the Enlightenment and of subsequent humanism was, as Peter Gay stated, that "philosophy was autonomous and omnipotent, or it was nothing."[8] Philosophy, then and there, began its modern departure from metaphysics and systematic thought to purely critical and analytical thought. Systematics in philosophy or theology implies for critical

---

5. ibid., p. 226.
6. St. Anselm, "Proslogium," in Sidney Norton Deane, trans., *St. Anselm: Proslogium; Monologium; An Appendix in Behalf of the Fool by Gaunilon and Cur Deus Homo* (Chicago, IL: Open Court Publishing Company, 1935), pp. 6–7.
7. Herman Dooyeweerd, *A New Critique of Theoretical Thought*, 4 vols. (Philadelphia, PA: Presbyterian and Reformed Publishing Co., 1953–1959).
8. Gay, *Enlightenment*, p. 236.

thought the tyranny of the absolute, of God, and hence true learning requires the rejection of systematics in favor of critical and autonomous thought.

It is impossible to understand modern education apart from this concept of the autonomy of critical thought, nor is it possible to have truly Christian education without a radical departure from that concept. As long as the educational curriculum functions consciously or unconsciously in terms of the autonomy of critical thought, the school remains, however evangelical its faculty, an implicitly anti-Christian institution.

Religiously, the implications of autonomous critical thought are far-reaching. As Van Til has summarized it,

> Modern man has his own substitute for historic Christianity. He, not God, determines the goal of life. He must be his own standard of right and wrong. He must provide his own motivation.[9]

According to Dewey, in *Experience and Education* (1938), the pupil must learn to set his own ideals in terms of himself as the criterion. For education, this means that the pupil's role is not one of acceptance in terms of a basic authority, and an intelligent development in terms of that authority, of the Christian faith and Christian scholarship. Rather, the pupil is an explorer, a discoverer, whose one authority is himself. The Christian scholar must sharpen his critical abilities, as he develops, in terms of bringing all facts to the bar of the sovereign and ontological Trinity and His Word. The autonomous man brings all factuality to the bar of his critical autonomy; no fact which challenges his sovereignty and autonomy can be permitted.

In the school, this means, *first* of all, that the pupil is a judge before he has any learning or wisdom. In fact, it is important that the very young child learn to view himself as judge and explorer before any system of thought subjugate his mind. The approach, therefore, is not to past learning in terms of appreciation and understanding, but in terms of critical analysis. On the college level, this becomes all the more explicit and vocal. In this writer's experience, the most despised and ridiculed professor at a

---

9. Cornelius Van Til, *The Dilemma of Education* (Grand Rapids, MI: National Union of Christian Schools, 1954), p. 2.

major university, in the English department, was a man whose approach to poetry was in terms of a traditional appreciation, enjoyment, and technical knowledge of music, meter, verse form, and the like. For most professors and students, this professor's unabashed enjoyment of great poetry was shameful: it lacked the framework of autonomous critical thought which is the hallmark of the modern intellectual.

The result has been, in literature, a steady replacement of older classics with newer works which are amenable to the critical spirit. An example of the disappearing classic is the ode by the Reverend Charles Wolfe, written in 1817, on "The Burial of Sir John Moore at Corunna."

> Not a drum was heard, not a funeral note,
>> As his corpse to the rampart we hurried;
> Not a soldier discharged his farewell shot
>> O'er the grave where our hero we buried.
>
> We buried him darkly at dead of night,
>> The sod with our bayonets turning,
> By the struggling moonbeam's misty light,
>> And the lanterns dimly burning.
>
> No useless coffin enclosed his breast,
>> Not in sheet nor in shroud we wound him;
> But he lay like a warrior taking his rest,
>> With his martial cloak around him.
>
> Few and short were the prayers we said,
>> And we spoke not a word of sorrow;
> But we steadfastly gazed on the face that was dead,
>> And we bitterly thought of the morrow.
>
> We thought, as we hollowed his narrow bed,
>> And smooth'd down his lonely pillow,
> That the foe and the stranger would tread o'er his head
>> And we far away on the billow!
>
> Lightly they'll talk of the spirit that's gone,
>> And o'er his cold ashes upbraid him —

But little he'll reck, if they let him sleep on
    In the grave where a Briton has laid him.

But half of our heavy task was done,
    When the clock struck the hour for retiring;
And we heard the distant and random gun
    That the foe was sullenly firing.

Slowly and sadly we laid him down,
    From the field of his fame, fresh and gory;
We carved not a line, and we raised not a stone—
    But we left him alone with his glory!

Wolfe's poem is a literal and accurate account of a military leader and hero, Sir John Moore, on the night before a British withdrawal. It is great poetry and accurate history. But the poem throughout moves in terms of a world of meaning which is now regarded as obsolete: a world of authority and faith, of prayer and courage, of patriotism and loyalty. The poem evokes emotions quite alien to the concept of the autonomy of critical thought. Like many another great poem, it is therefore eliminated from textbooks and popular anthologies, and college majors in English can graduate without even knowing of the existence of such poems.

The modern mood is one of "alienation" from "a world I never made." The rebellion against reality is not premised on a horror for sin and the fall, against one's own depravity, nor is it a longing for more grace. Rather, it is "alienation" from a world man did not create and a demand that man become his own maker. Charles G. Bell speaks of

Houseless home of our wanderings—vacant fields
And tall inhuman cities.[10]

For these men, God's world is the world of nothingness, so that Archibald MacLeish, in "The End of the World," sees its end thus:

There in the sudden blackness, the black pall of nothing,
nothing, nothing—nothing at all.[11]

---

10. Charles G. Bell, "From Le Havre," in Rolfe Humphries, ed., *New Poems* (New York, NY: Ballantine Books, 1953), p. 18.
11. Louis Untermeyer, ed., *The Concise Treasury of Great Poems* (Garden City, NY:

More recently, modern poetry and prose has abandoned meaning in favor of expression and has abandoned sentence structure and logical context. Some of its essentials are, according to Jack Kerouac, "Beat" writer,

Submission to everything, open, listening—
. . . .
Write what you want bottomless from bottom of the mind
The unspeakable visions of the individual
No time for poetry but exactly what is—
. . . .
Remove literary, grammatical and syntactical inhibition
. . . .
No fear or shame in the dignity of yr experience, language and knowledge
Composing wild, undisciplined, pure, coming in from under, crazier the better
You're a Genius all the time.[12]

In this concept of writing, the ability of the writer is implicitly in direct ratio to his abandonment of all authority other than his own experience. This abandonment requires the condemnation of God's authority in the name of the individual's authority.

Second, since experience is emphasized, and this experience is *private* experience, it is by implication *lawless* experience. Since it must be from the "bottom of the mind," and since the autonomy of critical thought requires a declaration of independence from God, it is necessary that autonomous experience be lawless. As a result, in literature the world of experience is increasingly criminal. The hero is the homosexual, the criminal, the psychopath, and, increasingly, the writer is also. Jean Genet is an ex-convict; Allen Ginsberg a former mental patient; both treat perversion as the new normality. This is increasingly the meaning of experience. Experience in godliness is not seen as true experience; it is subjection to authority. Experience in stealing is educative and independent. Hence, there is a literary cultivation of such experience, and in the beatnik, hippie, and other movements, the cultivation by students and ex-students of this true

Permabooks, [1942] 1953), p. 497.
12. Thomas Parkinson, ed., *A Casebook on the Beat* (New York, NY: Thomas Y. Crowell Company, 1961), pp. 67–68.

world of experience.

This emphasis on private experience carries over even into science, where Eddington has defined "the modern scientific philosophy" as "selective subjectivism":

> Selective subjectivism, which is the modern scientific philosophy, has little affinity with Berkeleian subjectivism, which, if I understand rightly, denies all objectivity to the external world. In our view the physical universe is neither wholly subjective nor wholly objective — nor a simple mixture of subjective and objective entities or attributes.[13]

In education, according to Dewey,

> It *is* the business of the school environment to eliminate, so far as possible, the unworthy features of the existing environment from influence on mental habitudes. It establishes a purified medium of action. Selection aims not only at simplifying but at weeding out what is undesirable. Every society gets encumbered with what is trivial, with dead wood from the past, and with what is positively perverse.[14]

This refined, purified experience means the elimination of Christian faith, the Bible, prayer, and worship. It means that the child is set into the "experiential continuum" in which no standard exists save the private experience and pragmatic considerations. The state school textbooks are written to foster this refined anti-Christian experience. The need in Christian education is for textbooks designed to further the Christian experience of reality in terms of the absolute sovereignty of God.

Third, the autonomy of critical thought is an educational philosophy which spells the death of educational, personal, and social progress. For critical thought, progress means the elimination of Christianity; it means man's "liberation" from the "tyranny" of God. Once Christianity is overthrown, *no direction* remains. Human welfare and human betterment are held to be social goals, but in the absence of norms, of objective standards, what is good, and what is bad? What constitutes better or worse? The sociologist Eugen Rosenstock-Huessy has called the contemporary relativism,

---

13. Sir Arthur Eddington, *The Philosophy of Physical Science* (New York, NY: Macmillan, 1939), p. 27.

14. John Dewey, *Experience and Education* (New York, NY: Macmillan, 1938), p. 29.

"Our Invasion by China." The stagnation of Asiatic civilization has been a product of relativism, of ancient pragmatism, of an abandonment of the concept of absolute truth, of an absolute moral law. "I suggest that the Theosophical Society has not imported into America one per cent of the Oriental thinking which has been introduced by pragmatism."[15] It is liberalism which leads to a static society, to the Chinafication of the West, by its relativism, by its assertion of the necessity for autonomous critical thought. This contemporary pragmatic faith Rosenstock-Huessy has summarized ably:

1. Society is God and otherwise there is no god who sends us into the world by calling us by our names.
2. Therefore, human speech is merely a tool, not an inspiration; a set of words, not a baptism of fire.
3. Society includes all men regardless of their evil character. Everybody can be educated, or reeducated. The body politic needs no self-purification.
4. The *ipse dixit* of authority is always out of place. Conflicts can be solved by discussions between equals.[16]

The revolution "of modern man is an attempt to move backward from Christ to Adam, to assert that the true grace of life is not in Christ but in the natural Adam, and the fallen Adam is seen as innocent in his rebellion and most truly in paradise when most rebellious."[17] The *philosophes* and the French Revolution sought to replace Christ with Adam. The concept of creativity was transferred from God to man.

Adam the digger, the chopper, but especially Adam the pioneer, is like the Creator, free and divine. Goethe expressed the new gospel when he wrote: "Allah need create no longer. We instead create his world."

In fact the word "creation" itself changed its meaning completely during the nineteenth century, at least in French, and to a certain extent in other languages too. The "derniere creation" of a fashion, and industry, can be

---

15. Eugen Rosenstock-Huessy, *The Christian Future: Or the Modern Mind Outrun* (New York, NY: Charles Scribner's Sons, 1946), p. 43.

16. ibid., p. 46.

17. Eugen Rosenstock-Huessy, *Out of Revolution: Autobiography of Western Man* (New York, NY: William Morrow, 1938).

advertised in this new world because man himself becomes the Promethean creator of a new earth organized by free human will. The "demiurge," the magic hero of antiquity, is turned into the "creative mind" of genius.[18]

For the Jacobins, "Adam became a great messianic figure standing for the end of time when all men should meet again."[19]

If man himself as Adam, governed only by the biology of his being, is his own god and paradise, then no progress is possible. Man becomes content with himself. His concept of life becomes static. But man, knowing himself to be totally depraved, and the world and himself in bondage to sin and death, knows also that the grace of God in Jesus Christ makes him victorious over sin and death. *Progress is therefore a moral necessity; it is sanctification.* The Biblical doctrine of sanctification is basic to the belief in progress.

A *fourth* consequence of the autonomy of critical thought is that education into critical thought becomes salvation. Education therefore becomes messianic.[20] The result is "government by textbooks," to use Rosenstock-Huessy's phrase. Every modern country, whether fascist, communist, socialist, or democratic, exercises control over textbooks in varying degrees, from indirect, to "dictatorial textbook administration."[21] The school becomes the church of the *philosophes*, the new intellectuals, by means of which the humanistic creed is to be catechized to the generations.

Between the Christian and the non-Christian perspectives, there is a vast intellectual and educational gulf. "The Christian position seeks to make human experience intelligible in terms of the presupposition of God; the non-Christian position seeks to make human experience intelligible in terms of man who is conceived of as ultimate."[22]

Some of the presuppositions of Christian education are: *first*, the sovereignty of God, and the authority of His infallible Word. Both sovereignty and infallibility are necessary and inescapable concepts. If they are denied

---

18. ibid., pp. 181–182.

19. ibid., p. 217.

20. See R. J. Rushdoony, *The Messianic Character of American Education* (Nutley, NJ: Craig Press, 1963).

21. Eugen Rosenstock-Huessy, *Out of Revolution*, p. 690.

22. Cornelius Van Til, *The Dilemma of Education*, p. 40.

to God, they accrue to man, or to some aspect of the universe or of history. The autonomy of critical thought is a concept asserting the sovereignty and, upon certain conditions, the infallibility of critical thought. There can be no compromise between these two positions.

Second, critical thought can better flourish within the context of Biblical Christianity than autonomous humanism. Autonomous critical thought is critical of God, of Christian faith, of the Scriptures, but not critical of man and the state. Where man and the state become humanistic, Christian critical thought is of necessity critical of man and the state because of its doctrine of sin. Autonomous critical thought moves to stifle such criticism because it is an attack on its presuppositions. There is thus a marked decline of philosophical thought as it progresses towards the conclusion of autonomous philosophy. Of this, pragmatism and existentialism are good examples. Christian education needs to emphasize Christian critical thought, a critique of man and society in terms of Biblical faith.

Third, Christian education is frankly and honestly authoritarian, but it must assert that *all* education is authoritarian. The basic question is always, *which authority, God or man?* Statist education today is education into *authoritarian humanism. The Christian school is frankly organized in terms of God's authority, and the ordained authorities God has given to man in family, church, state, school, and society.*

Fourth, Christian education must assert at all times the absolute law of God. For autonomous critical thought, the only absolute law is man's freedom from God. For the Christian, every sphere of life, the family, church, state, economics, agriculture, science, mathematics, and all things else, are under God's absolute laws as manifested in their sphere. Christian education is a study of God's grace, of God's realms of law. Conflicts are thus not "solved by discussions," but by the objective study of and reference to God's world of law. The fact that man's reaction to and study of that realm of law is subjective, makes all the more necessary the exercise of Christian critical thought to avoid the confusion of man's experiential framework with objective reality. The fact of man's sin always conditions man's experience, but, because man is not ultimate, reality is not governed by man's experience. Man either learns, or he suffers for his warped or erroneous knowledge. Moreover, since man was created by the same God who created all reality, man's being is governed by the same world of law, purpose, and meaning, which governs the whole of creation. Man's subjective experience is thus not alien to reality but a part thereof and understandable in terms of God's law. Man himself witnesses to God against himself. The reality around man and within man can only be truly known in terms of the sovereign God Who created all things. The fear of the Lord is the beginning of all instruction and learning.

Fifth, the purpose of Christian education is not academic: it is religious and practical. Man's purpose is to build the Kingdom of God.[23] This was Adam's calling, the creation mandate, the call to man to know, subdue, and use the earth under God. As Hills has written,

> *Be fruitful, and multiply, and replenish the earth, and subdue it: and have dominion over the fish of the sea, and over the fowl of the air*, was God's program for the world and for the human race. This was the mandate which He gave them. It was God's will that Adam and his posterity should erect upon earth a sinless civilization and culture the splendor of which we cannot now have even the faintest conception. A civilization without sin and suffering, a civilization in which every gift of God would be used properly and to the fullest advantage, a civilization of perfect physical, mental, and spiritual health, a civilization in which death would be unknown. Such would be the civilization and culture which would exist today if Adam had been obedient to the divine commandment.[24]

In the providence of God, man turned instead to Satan's plan for his kingdom of autonomy from God. In Satan's plan, every man would be his own god, knowing, that is, determining for himself in terms of his own wishes, what constitutes good and evil (Gen. 3:5). Autonomous critical thought had to be exercised against God, according to Satan: "Yea, hath God said?" (Gen. 3:1). Through Jesus Christ, God's second Adam, God's plan was reestablished, and the program for God's Kingdom announced to all nations, who were summoned to discipleship under Christ (Matt. 28:19–20). The task of Christian education is to obey and to further God's program in terms of His calling and Word.

---

23. ibid., p. 41.

24. Edward F. Hills, *Believing Bible Study* (Des Moines, IA: Christian Research Press, 1967), p. 101.

Chapter 4

THE CURRICULUM & THE RESURRECTION

As WE HAVE seen, a liberal arts curriculum is a course or path in the arts of freedom. Since the doctrine of the resurrection of Jesus Christ is a witness to the defeat of sin and death, and the restoration of the redeemed man in Christ to dominion, it follows that the fact of the resurrection is central to a liberal arts curriculum. St. Paul speaks of "the power of his resurrection" (Phil. 3:10). "'The power,' or *efficacy*, 'of His resurrection' is the justification, and regeneration inseparable from it, which lie at the entrance of Christian life."[1] According to Lenski,

> This power of Christ's resurrection became Paul's personal blessed *gnosis*. He was made to know Christ Jesus as "his Lord" (v. 8), for Jesus appeared to Paul to bring him to contrition and to faith, not to damn him with his omnipotence.
>
> "The power of his resurrection" means that by the resurrection he was made both Lord and Christ (Acts 5:31), made unto us wisdom and *righteousness* and sanctification and ransoming (I Cor. 1:30). "The power of his resurrection" is the seal of his redemption. God accepted his ransom by raising Christ and by glorifying him so that all who by faith embrace this Christ who died and rose again for our justification (Rom. 4:24, 25) are justified by God, have "the righteousness from God on the basis of faith" (v. 9). This is "the surpassingness of the knowledge of Christ Jesus, *my Lord.*"[2]

This "power of the resurrection" is the foundation of the Christian life.

---

1. Alfred Barry, "Philippians," in C. J. Ellicott, *Ellicott's Commentary on the Whole Bible*, vol. 8 (Grand Rapids, MI: Zondervan, n.d.), p. 82.

2. R. C. H. Lenski, *The Interpretation of St. Paul's Epistles to the Galatians, to the Ephesians and to the Philippians* (Minneapolis, MN: Augsburg, [1937] 1961), pp. 841–842.

It involves not only power but also resurrection, not only a new and redeemed life in Christ but also a growth in terms of the principle of the resurrection. The fall of man was into sin and death; the redemption of man is into righteousness and life *towards a purpose.*

A humanistic and relativistic education has no transcendental frame of reference; it has no goal or purpose outside of man. Education then has as its goal education for man's sake, for a better society for man. The problem then arises: who shall determine what is best for all mankind? Is this determined by a consensus or by a majority vote? If so, what about the 49 percent, or 1 percent, who dissent from the majority? Education then ceases to be for their sake except by imposition and coercion. A humanistic philosophy of education alternates between anarchism and totalitarianism. It can assert an independence not only of men but of areas of study: art for art's sake, knowledge for knowledge's sake, pure scientific research as apart from pragmatic and industrial research, and so on. What determines, then, the value of such an approach? A bare assertion, an act of faith, is all that is involved. Moreover, the purely existentialist purpose is really no purpose at all but rather whim. *Purpose* implies transcendence, a goal to be attained, an inadequacy in the present situation or condition of man, and therefore a determination to reach a superior place. The word comes from *pro*, before, *pono*, place, and it is thus a call for man to go beyond himself to an established goal. In an existentialist world, purpose in this true sense of the word is impossible, in that motivation is purely out of the biology of man and the impulses of the moment, unconditioned by prior goals, religious instruction, or social expectations. The result is that *whim* then governs man, a "sudden, unexpected, and unreasonable deviation of the mind from its usual or natural course; caprice; freak."

A Christian liberal arts curriculum is therefore a purposive curriculum in terms of the doctrine of the resurrection and the calling of man to exercise dominion and to subdue the earth. Certain requirements are therefore basic to a curriculum which is based on sound theology.

First, the student must be enabled to grow in his dominion over himself as a necessary first step towards exercising dominion over the earth. A humanistic curriculum can be, as we have noted, either totalitarian or anarchistic. It can suppress the student or use him merely as a social resource to be used by the state, or it can allow him an anarchistic self-expression which is destructive of both learning and discipline.

According to Proverbs 22:6, "Train up a child in the way he should go: and when he is old, he will not depart from it." Kidner comments:

> The training prescribed is lit. "according to his (the child's) way," imply-ing, it seems, respect for his individuality and vocation, though not for his selfwill (see verse 5, or 14:12).
>
> But the stress is on parental opportunity and duty. *Train* means elsewhere to "dedicate" a house (Dt. 20:5), temple (I Ki. 8:63), etc. Possibly a trace of this meaning clings to it.[3]

Fritsch also calls attention to the fact that *train* elsewhere means "to dedi-cate," while not seeing it as so intended here.[4] There is no good reason to deny the validity of the basic meaning of "to dedicate"; the text requires that we dedicate a child to the way of his individuality and vocation under God. To dedicate means to set apart or to devote. The purpose of educa-tion is in part a separation and a devotion of the student in terms of his aptitudes and abilities. It means also a discipline in the same direction. An important aspect of education is to provide a child with an opportunity to find his aptitudes and calling and to develop himself in terms of them.

There can be no dominion without the tools of dominion. A student who comes to know his aptitudes and is disciplined in the use of them is clearly prepared for dominion over himself and over the world.

Clearly, too, the basic tool of dominion is a knowledge of Scripture. As a result, the teaching of the Bible is a basic part of a Christian curriculum in order that the child can have the finest discipline and guidance directly from Scripture rather than second hand. The results of such teaching are highly productive of a self-disciplined character. The Reverend T. Rob-ert Ingram reports a delightful story in this connection. At St. Thomas Episcopal School in Houston, Texas, children in the early grades memo-rize proverb after proverb, until the whole book of Proverbs is committed to memory. On one occasion, third-grade boys were on the playground,

---

3. Derek Kidner, *Proverbs: An Introduction and Commentary* (Chicago, IL: Inter-Varsity Press, 1964), p. 147.

4. Charles T. Fritsch, "Proverbs," in *The Interpreter's Bible*, vol. 4 (New York, NY: Abingdon Press, 1955), p. 907.

when a teacher confronted one boy with an offense committed earlier. The guilty boy immediately pointed to a second boy, saying, he made me do it. At this point, a third boy stepped up and remarked, "My son, if sinners entice thee, consent thou not" (Prov. 1:10). This is, of course, one of the advantages of a knowledge of Scripture: it enables us to understand ourselves and others, as well as to know God.

Second, a Christian liberal arts curriculum should enable the student to exercise dominion over the world. The purpose of the Christian school should be to prepare generation after generation to dominate every area of life and thought. A monastic education is not Christian. It is not the legitimate purpose of the Christian school to prepare the child or student for a retreat from the world. Too often, however, this is the case with "evangelical" churches and schools. The student is summoned to withdraw from the world into a cloistered area in which the person is insulated from the problems of the world. Usually, the evangelical student groups at many colleges and universities are the most difficult of all groups to speak to. Some of the students have drifted into a compromising neutralism. Others accept the faith of the world, and they attempt to combine, for example, creationism and evolution, and are unwilling to hear an uncompromising statement of Christian faith, or they have retreated into a sterile pietism which substitutes prayers and the singing of childish choruses for systematic theological thinking. Not surprisingly, many "evangelical" conference grounds are now being called, or their sessions are called, *retreats*; the term has been borrowed from monastic life, and it means that Protestantism has surrendered all too extensively its militancy for pietistic retreat.

The student must be schooled to see every legitimate area as an area of necessary dominion. He must be taught that the people of God must assert the crown rights of King Jesus over every area of life. There can be no compromise nor any diminution of this goal.

A relativistic philosophy will ultimately work to destroy every area of knowledge. By destroying meaning, it will destroy the validity of study and research, as even a non-Christian scientist has observed.[5]

5. Gunther S. Stent, *The Coming of the Golden Age: A View of the End of Progress* (Garden City, NY: The Natural History Press, 1969).

Third, the goal of Christian education cannot be exhaustive knowledge but rather principled knowledge. According to Van Til,

> The Westminster Shorter Catechism asks, "How does Christ execute the office of a prophet?" The answer is: "Christ executeth the office of a Prophet, in revealing to us by his Word and Spirit, the will of God for our salvation." Now, if we recall that man set for himself a false ideal of knowledge when he became a sinner, that is, he lost true wisdom, we may say that in Christ man was reinstated to true knowledge. In Christ man realized that he is a creature of God and that he cannot seek for comprehensive knowledge. Christ is our wisdom. He is our wisdom not only in the sense that he tells us how to get to heaven; he is our wisdom too in teaching us true knowledge about everything concerning which we should have knowledge.[6]

In the world of brute factuality of humanistic man, the only possibility of true knowledge is where exhaustive knowledge exists, an impossibility. This means that knowledge is an impossibility on humanistic terms, and only a pragmatic and instrumental use of factuality can exist. However, even this perishes quickly, because, without a purpose and without meaning, the pragmatic and instrumentalist approaches have no frame of reference and hence collapse.

Because of this devotion to exhaustive knowledge, the universities of the past century have multiplied courses. In part, this proliferation within the curriculum has been an aspect of academic empire building, but its rationale has been the goal of exhaustive knowledge. Supposedly, the more courses a university offers, the more adequately it prepares a student for life. As a result, it is not uncommon for a university with 30,000 students to have many courses attended by one to five students only. In a few cases, these courses are perhaps necessary, as witness a course in cuneiform, or Assyrian language, but, in most cases, the student could learn the same things on his own, and more quickly, in another course, or without a teacher. Such courses, however, are regarded as the essence of a university and its prestige. They are imitated by many if not all colleges, and they are not without their influence on elementary and secondary education.

---

6. Cornelius Van Til, *The Defense of the Faith* (Philadelphia, PA: Presbyterian and Reformed Publishing Co., 1955), p. 33.

To emphasize as against this a basic curriculum with a perspective on knowledge rather than specialization in a multiplicity of fields, is to go against the trend of twentieth-century education. All the same, a principled education must be stressed as the only Christian method. Moreover, it must be asserted that the exhaustive method is dishonest. It supposedly defers all principles until all the facts are in, and it claims to be scientific and objective thereby. It does not, however, defer principles; it begins with the principle that there is no God, and of the ultimacy of autonomous man. Thus, the principle it believes an exhaustive knowledge will disclose is made the basis of operation at the beginning of its study. As against this patent dishonesty and deceit, the Christian must begin with an open avowal of faith in the triune God of Scripture and His infallible Word, and in the fact that "all things were made by him; and without him was not any thing made that was made" (John 1:3), so that no fact can be truly known apart from Him. As against this open act of faith, humanism begins with an avowal of pure research before principles are formulated, whereas in fact it predetermines those principles by an initial act of faith.

Fourth, turning again to Van Til, we read, concerning the office of Christ as priest,

> Again, the catechism asks: "How does Christ execute the office of a Priest?" The answer is: "Christ executeth the office of a Priest, in his once offering up himself a sacrifice to satisfy divine justice, and reconcile us to God, and in making continual intercession for us." We need not discuss this point except to indicate that Christ's work as priest cannot be separated from his work as prophet. Christ could not give us true knowledge of God and of the universe unless he *died* for us as priest. The question of knowledge is an ethical question at root. It is indeed possible to have theoretically correct knowledge about God without loving God. The devil illustrates this point. Yet what is meant by knowing God in Scripture is *knowing and loving* God: this is true knowledge of God: the other is *false*.[7]

Christ by His atonement restores the elect to true knowledge, as Van Til has so extensively demonstrated; "The question of knowledge is an ethical question at root." Man in rebellion against God is in rebellion against

---

7. ibid., p. 33.

the very foundation of all true knowledge, and this fact must be basic to Christian education. No neutrality is possible, because there are no neutral facts in the universe, only God-created facts. Men either accept God's interpretation, or they attempt as their own gods to create their own universe of meaning (Gen. 3:5).

The Christian school cannot take over the function of the church: it is not an agency for revivalism, evangelism, or attempts at conversion. Its function is education. It must be insisted, however, that, when the Christian school is faithful to its calling, it makes as telling a witness as any church ever has. The relationship of noetics to ethics, of knowing to morality, is normally regarded in pagan terms: it is held that man's supposedly autonomous reason is able to discern and to know reality without reference to his ethical status, i.e., without reference to the fact that he is a sinner, or a redeemed man. As against this, the orthodox Christian approach is that man's knowledge rests on a common religious premise with his ethical concepts. Man's entire outlook is colored and determined by the fact that he is either a covenant-keeper or a covenant-breaker with God.[8] The Christian school, by stressing the noetic effect of sin, cuts the ground out from under unbelief and makes clear the grounds of true knowledge.

Of the office of Christ as king, the catechism reads, "Christ executeth the office of a King, in subduing us to himself, in ruling and defending us, and in restraining and conquering all of his and our enemies." Van Til here comments,

> Again we observe that this work of Christ as king must be brought into organic connection with his work as prophet and priest. To give us true wisdom or knowledge Christ must subdue us. He died for us to *subdue* us and thus gave us wisdom. It is only by emphasizing this organic connection of the aspects of the work of Christ that we can avoid all mechanical separation of the intellectual and the moral aspects of the question of knowledge.[9]

We have already discussed man's dominion over himself, which is a product of Christ's dominion over us. A further fact needs to be noted: a basic premise of the humanistic rejection of the knowledge of God as first

---

8. See R. J. Rushdoony, *The One and the Many* (Nutley, NJ: Craig Press, 1971), pp. 192–196.
9. Van Til, *Defense of the Faith*, pp. 33–34.

principle, in favor of man's autonomous mind as first principle on a quest for exhaustive knowledge, has been this aphorism: knowledge is power. The meaning is that, as against God's omnipotence and omniscience, when man gains more and more knowledge towards the goal of exhaustive knowledge, he will gain power to a proportionate degree. With this, the orthodox Christian must dissent, holding rather that godly, principled knowledge gives power, in that it enables us to better understand and use God's creation under God and to His glory. The purpose of Christian education is thus very frankly to enlarge the scope and extent of man's power under God. Power is not to be decried but to be used. The enemies of Christian education know its potential for power, and, with a world at stake, are determined to destroy it. Christian schools need to develop and expand the potential for power in Christian education.

Part II

Chapter 1

HISTORY VERSUS SOCIAL SCIENCE

INCREASINGLY, IN THE twentieth-century schools, the teaching of history has either given way to or been radically infected by the concept of social science. The approach of the social sciences to history, or to any field of study, is governed by two basic premises. *First*, history and society must be studied scientifically, that is, in terms of purely naturalistic considerations, without reference to God or to any eternal law. This methodology of necessity requires ultimately a materialistic philosophy of history. The presupposition of this methodology is anti-Christian. God, and a Christian purpose and meaning, are denied to history. The motive force of history can only be from within history. *Second*, since the scientific method gives paramount importance to experiment, a scientific society must be an experiment in scientific planning. Since controls are basic to experimentation, in order to produce a valid result, a totalitarian society is the goal of the social sciences, in that freedom is destructive to planning and human engineering. The social sciences therefore are hostile to freedom in any historic Christian sense. Freedom has no place in the laboratory of society.

History taught as a social science is therefore the story of man's struggle to liberate himself from God and superstition, and to find himself in terms of science, in independence of God and heaven, and a life lived in terms of exclusively this-worldly considerations. Modern history texts are written as the story of man's evolution upward to the liberating world of science.

Thus, a particularly well-written history text for high school world history, introduces itself to the students by declaring, "To pack a suitcase for a journey is more fun than to fill a box with odds and ends and put it in storage. When you prepare for a journey you have a *purpose*." What, then, is the purpose of world history? "The courses you take in school are part of the baggage you pack for the most important journey of all—your life." With reference to world history specifically, "In this course you will survey the march of humanity from earliest times to the present and learn about the great triumphs and tragedies of mankind. In other words, you will make human experience available to you."[1] For the authors, there is no law beyond man; the autonomy of critical thought is a basic assumption, and the only source of law is man. One of the conclusions of the book is a summary statement concerning law. The Ten Commandments are seen humanistically as designed to forbid "acts that would spread discord within the group." Earlier, "all laws were believed to be divine commands or revelations." The modern era changed that.

> Later, with the growth of democracy, people chose their own governments, governments that derived "their just powers from the consent of the governed." The laws of a state thus became an expression of the collective will and conscience of the citizens. But the highest purpose of law and religion remained the same: to promote the welfare, the harmony, and the cooperation of men in society.[2]

This "highest purpose of law and religion" is clearly and obviously humanism. The writers, in fact, see no other purpose. In the *Teacher's Manual*, the "Up-to-date Objectives of the World History Course in the High School Curriculum" are clearly spelled out, so that the teacher will not fail to understand and teach in terms of this basic humanism:

1. To see that many types of problems facing mankind have been persistent through the ages in various cultures.
2. To realize that the pace of change in human affairs has been accelerated throughout history, exemplified most vividly by the changes in the nineteenth and twentieth centuries.
3. To appreciate that the cooperative efforts of ever-larger groups have advanced civilization, and that the breakdown of cooperation and a resulting disunity have been backward steps in the history of mankind.

---

1. Geoffrey Bruun and Millicent Haines, *The World Story* (Boston, MA: D.C. Heath, 1963), p. 3.
2. ibid., p. 582.

4. To understand the significance of man's increasing control of his environment — the enormous benefits, the great responsibilities, and the grave dangers.

5. To know about and to understand the development of other nations and regions of the world, with which we now have such close contact, so that we may have a fuller appreciation of contemporary world problems.

6. To gain a background for understanding the decisions that our government now must make which in turn affect all parts of the globe.

7. To appreciate the strength of endurance that mankind has had to experience in order to achieve his present status.[3]

It should be noted that this textbook is far more conservative than most in its political perspective, although its view is clearly one of political and economic interventionism.[4] However, secular textbooks, whether conservative or radical, are agreed in their basic humanism. For Haines as well as all other writers of statist textbooks, *man makes history*. Primary determination is in man's hand, for better or worse.

From the Biblical perspective, God is the determiner of history. The young reformer Martin Luther reflected on the events he was engaged in and declared,

> God alone is in this business; we are seized — so that I see we are acted upon rather than act.[5]

Looking back twenty years later, he again asserted that everything had happened by divine counsel. For Luther, history is the work of God. Headley's excellent summary of Luther's view of history gives the Biblical position clearly:

> With his conviction that God is the ground of historical causation, Luther stands within the tradition of Paul and Augustine; only God could be at the root of all temporal events. At the same time the theocentric position separates him from modern historical understanding. This difference is not

---

3. Millicent Haines, *Teacher's Manual to Accompany Bruun-Haines, The World Story* (Boston, MA: D. C. Heath, 1963), p. 2.

4. ibid., pp. 79–80.

5. John M. Headly, *Luther's View of Church History* (New Haven, CT: Yale University Press, 1963), p. 1.

limited to the problem of causation but appears in its two immediate implications: that every action derived from God gives unity and meaning to history, and secondly, because man is the instrument of God one is denied the luxury of being a spectator. Man is constantly being acted upon and serves as a cooperator in this action. This unbroken activity of God pushes man into an unbroken cooperation in history. In such a situation there can be no dead history and no flight from history.[6]

These two perspectives are mutually exclusive: either God is God, or man is God, and history is either basically God's work or it is man's work. The Christian teaching of history cannot halt between these two opinions. History is not a social science; it is a theological science, because it is an aspect of God's creation.

The Christian view of history, as it appeared very early, saw the world outside of Christ as darkness. Christians were fully aware of the achievements of ancient cultures, but they were also intensely aware of their degeneracies and their willful rebellion against God. As a result, Christian historiography termed everything outside of Christ the "dark ages." Petrarch removed the term "Dark Ages" from classical, pre-Christian times to call the thousand years of Christianity by that title.[7] The Renaissance and subsequent humanism accepted this term happily, and, although it later limited the centuries so termed, humanism held basically to a concept of Christianity as darkness. Humanism and science were equated with light, so that, only with the nineteenth century, the dawn of Darwinianism and secular education, was the light seen as coming into its own.

The question, of course, is what constitutes light, and what constitutes darkness? If it is technology, the ancient engineers were often amazingly skilled in this respect.[8] But more was involved in "light" than these things. The "Middle Ages" were marked by no small social progress and architectural genius, and the earlier era saw a remarkable flowering of inventive genius and application.[9]

6. ibid., pp. 1–2.

7. Gay, *The Enlightenment*, p. 74.

8. L. Sprague De Camp, *The Ancient Engineers* (Garden City, NY: Anchor Books, 1960).

9. William Carroll Bark, *Origins of the Medieval World* (Garden City, NY: Anchor Books, 1960).

But for the modern mind, the key to "light," to true historiography, is the secularization of history in terms of the autonomy of critical thought. "Light" means unbelief; the reaction of educators to "hippie" culture is more congenial than to orthodox Christianity. Anti-Christianity in its every form is viewed as an aspect of "light," whereas Biblical faith means the "dark ages."

Christian education cannot view the modern era in its own light. It must be seen as a dark age, a period of growing unbelief in the God of Scripture, a time of rising statism and totalitarianism, an age of sometimes comfortable slavery which is inescapably slavery still.

The effect of evolutionary thinking on historiography has been very great. One of its central products is the stage theory of development. Variations of this theory appear in a variety of thinkers, in Marx, Spengler, and Voegelin. The various stages of historical development are marked by a "leap in being," or by a new phase of law as the current law of their being, or by the organismic limitations of a particular stage of growth. Instead of an objective law, there is an immanent law which is expressive of the historical moment. Feudalism worked because it was expressive of that stage of development, and capitalism worked as the law of another stage in man's development, and no overall law governs all things save a change premised on dialectical materialism or a related philosophy. Each society is "right" in terms of its own stage of growth. Thus Claude Levi-Strauss, French anthropologist, has declared, "A primitive people is not a backward or retarded people; indeed it may possess a genius for invention or action that leaves the achievements of civilized peoples far behind." This scholar's basic premise is a rejection of the concept of truth, and this he likes in savage societies. "What primitive man seeks above all is not truth but coherence; not the scientific distinction between true and false but a vision of the world that will satisfy his soul."[10] The Christian can agree that the savage is not a primitive; he is like all men a child of Adam. His problem is not primitivism but degeneracy. To equate the Christian cultures with those of Africa, and to demand appreciation of Africa's past and present, as many textbooks, including Bruun-Haines, do, is to ask us to endorse

---

10. Claude Levi-Strauss, "Man's New Dialogue With Man," *Time*, June 30, 1967, pp. 34–35.

and accept degeneracy. Such an approach converts Africa from a mission field desperately in need of God's saving grace into a sister-culture of equal dignity and character. *To accept this premise is to reject Christianity.* As a matter of fact, Levi-Strauss's ostensible catholicity of acceptance is very clearly a rejection of Christian civilization and the concept of truth, as *Tristes Tropiques* makes clear.[11] In commending his savages, Levi-Strauss is damning Christian culture and its concern for the truth.

In its every form, the stage theory of development is relativistic, and the further this concept is developed, the more radically does its relativism govern it. Levi-Strauss simply pressed his Marxist and existentialist presuppositions to their logical conclusion.

Thus, as we have seen, *first*, for Christian historiography, history is not a social science; it is a theological science. *Second*, it is a theological science because God, not man, is the sovereign lord of all creation. *Third*, the dark ages of history are therefore the non-Christian eras and areas, because Jesus Christ is the light of the world. The basic criterion of light is thus Christ, not science. *Fourth*, Christian historiography rests on the concept of absolute truth, a personal truth, Jesus Christ, and it is thus hostile to historical relativism. Its attitude towards pagan cultures is not one of appreciation but of evangelism. The Christian must oppose teaching designed to foster world brotherhood on humanistic terms. His standard remains: *not appreciation but evangelism.*

Fifth, for the Christian historian and teacher, the basic textbook is the Bible. History is viewed from its perspective. Moreover, the Bible gives us the one valid chronology for ancient history. The whole of the Old Testament gives us a meticulous, precise, and extensive account of genealogies which are a part of the inspired and infallible text. We need to be reminded of that fact, since the tendency to underrate or overlook the genealogical tables is so great. But they plainly give us a chronology for world history. Philip Mauro noted, some years ago,

In other words, if we take it that the lifetime of mankind has been something less than six thousand years (and there is no evidence at all for a longer

---

11. Claude Levi-Strauss, *A World on the Wane*, trans. John Russell, with four chap. omitted (New York, NY: Criterion Books, 1961).

term of human experience) then we have the remarkable fact that for about *three-fifths of the entire period* there is no chronological information whatever *except in the Bible*; whereas, on the other hand, during that same period (wherein other records are, as regards chronology, a perfect blank) the chronology of the Bible is most definite and complete.[12]

A belief in the Bible cannot be taught if we fail to take it seriously in its every aspect. The Bible gives not merely a chronology of history, but the meaning, purpose, and direction of history. History is governed, not by the philosophies' "omnipotence of criticism,"[13] but by the omnipotence of the triune God. It cannot be understood apart from Him and His Word.

---

12. Philip Mauro, *The Wonders of Bible Chronology* (Swengel, PA: Bible Truth Depot, 1961), p. 4. Mauro relied basically on the work of Martin Anstey, *The Romance of Bible Chronology*, 2 vols. (London, England: Marshall Brothers, 1913). Alfred M. Rehwinkel follows the Septuagint to give a somewhat older date for creation; see *The Age of the Earth and Chronology of the Bible* (Adelaide, South Australia: Lutheran Publishing House, 1967). For the chronology of the Hebrew kings, see Edwin R. Thiele, *The Mysterious Numbers of the Hebrew Kings*, rev. ed. (Grand Rapids, MI: William B. Eerdmans, revised edition, 1965).

13. Gay, *The Enlightenment*, p. 145.

Chapter 2

TEACHING BIBLE

BIBLE CLASSES IN a Christian school are a failure, unless the essentials of Biblical faith are applied to every course in the school. I have visited supposedly strong fundamentalist colleges over the past twenty years and seen why they were destined to drift into neo-orthodoxy and into evolutionary thinking by looking at the non-Biblical courses. In several cases, this drift is already very much in evidence. The reason for it is that, for example, mathematics is taught from a relativistic view point; classes begin with prayer, and then instruction implicitly denies God. The science courses presuppose a universe which is an impersonal and blind force, not the creation of the personal God. Sociology and social studies courses assume that predestination is in man's hand, not God's. Psychology and anthropology, instead of being branches of theology, as they were in origin, are made the handmaids of humanism, and so on. A humanistic curriculum cannot be made Christian by introductory prayers or by a sprinkling of holy water, but only by means of clear-cut Biblical presuppositions.

The Bible, as Cornelius Van Til has pointed out, does not give us the multiplicity of facts which make up mathematics, paleontology, physics, biology, or any other subject, but it does give us *the truth about all facts.* It declares all facts to be God-created, God-governed, and God-serving facts.

The Bible is *basic to all of education* because it gives us *the meaning of all facts and the purpose of education.* Solomon makes two important statements with respect to instruction:

> The fear of the LORD is the beginning of knowledge: but fools despise wisdom and instruction. (Prov. 1:7)

44

The fear of the LORD is the beginning of wisdom: and the knowledge of the holy is understanding. (Prov. 9:10)

There is an important difference between *knowledge* and *wisdom*. Both are commended by Scripture. Knowledge is one aspect of the image of God in man (Col. 3:10; Gen. 2:19–20). Knowledge, however, apart from God becomes mere learning. The extent of learning in the modern world is great, but it is like the learning of Alexandria, meaningless and without focus. A doctoral dissertation on Shakespeare's use of commas gives us much learning; we acquire extensive and minute knowledge, but little, if any, wisdom. Wisdom, on the other hand, is insight and understanding. Knowledge and wisdom are united in a Christian faith which is Biblical and must be united in Christian education. St. Paul's counsel to Timothy makes a like emphasis:

Study to shew thyself approved unto God, a workman that needeth not to be ashamed, rightly dividing the word of truth. But shun profane and vain babblings: for they will increase unto more ungodliness. (2 Tim. 2:15–16)

The "vain (or futile) babblings" are speculations which are pointless and are motivated by curiosity rather than wisdom. Some men try endlessly to read new knowledge out of Scripture on heaven, hell, angels, and demons. They want curious information, not wisdom. Much current research and scholarship in the liberal arts and sciences similarly lacks wisdom.

Teaching the Bible should be done with knowledge and wisdom. The Bible is God's revelation to man; it has as its purpose the communication by God to man of God's purpose and salvation. In teaching the Bible, it should be remembered, *first*, that the Christian school is a school, not a church. Its essential function is education, not evangelism. The two must not be confused. In some schools, the goal of the Bible class is conversion; as a result, instruction suffers, and grading tends to be in terms of a response rather than a solid knowledge of Scripture. The teacher's job is to instruct and to grade; the evangelist's function is to present the plan of salvation with conviction and regeneration as the goal. The evangelist's "grading" is different. The best foundation for evangelization is laid by solid instruction. Scripture declares, "faith cometh by hearing, and hearing by the word of God" (Rom. 10:17). There is no better human instrument possible to assure a hearing ear than the Christian school and sound Bible classes therein.

Second, the class should be given a clear-cut overview of Biblical history and doctrine. Most Sunday school instruction is almost useless, because the average child has little sense of the unity of Scripture or of Bible chronology. Sunday school instruction is usually full of gimmicks to command interest, is a form of babysitting, and is too often a disaster to Christ's cause. The Christian school must make the Bible class, above all, highly disciplined and thorough.

Third, Christian education can never be abstract. The goal of humanistic education is abstraction. Reality being impersonal, the truth about reality for the humanist is not concrete and implicit and explicit in factuality. For us, all facts are concrete and personal facts created by God; they have the meaning God gave them. It is not necessary to abstract a meaning in terms of their imposed meaning as given by man. An abstraction analyzes the potential significance of a thing and concludes, in terms of a humanistic framework, what meaning can be ascribed to that meaningless void. Humanism, as it approaches the Bible, seeks to mine it for some possible ore of meaning useful to modern man. Some churchmen who claim to be Bible-believers do the same. They write or talk about "nuggets from the book of Joshua." This cannot be our approach. God's meaning in Joshua must be our meaning, not an abstraction. Thus, we must make certain that our study of Joshua begins with the commission, Joshua 1:2–9; it is succeeded in Scripture by the Great Commission of Matthew 28:18–20, which summarizes it. Joshua and Israel must go forth and conquer the land of Canaan for the Lord; the church as God's New Israel must conquer the world for Christ; and so on.

Our study thus must be historical and concrete. This also means that it then best fulfills God's purpose. Solomon, in speaking of the goads and nails of teaching, says, "Let us hear the conclusion of the whole matter: Fear God, and keep his commandments: for this is the whole duty of man" (Eccles. 12:13). We teach the Bible; we teach the plan of salvation therein, and the way of salvation. We *teach*: the rest is left to the Holy Spirit and the ministry of the Word.

Then, *fourth,* we must always remember that the Bible is not only the Word of God but also the most exciting book there is. Our teaching should not deaden the excitement, beauty, and power of the Bible.

An illustration of a common obliviousness to this aspect of Scripture comes from a pre-World War II England. In a school chapel, the daily readings followed the Episcopal lectionary, which divides Acts 27 into several readings, i.e., Acts 27:1–26 for the Wednesday of the fourth Sunday after Trinity, Acts 27:27 for Thursday, Acts 27:14 on the ninth Sunday after Trinity, and so on. A boy without a Christian background, or else no knowledge of Scripture, was asked to read Acts 27:1–26. He continued to read beyond the appointed text. When the headmaster attempted to stop him, the boy told him to be quiet, because he wanted to see what happened. Would there be a shipwreck, and would the passengers be saved? The boy was reading the Bible intelligently. Too often, we ask people to study it in unintelligent terms, as though it were not a remarkably stirring book.

Fifth, the Bible should be read and studied as the Word of the living God, an infallible and inerrant Word, because no other Word is possible from the sovereign and omniscient God. It is this book that governs Christian education and the Christian school. The teacher must grow in terms of that book in order to teach it properly. If our understanding of the Bible does not grow continually, we are not competent to teach the Bible. Only those who feel its power and excitement can communicate it, and only those who know the God of Scripture can teach the truth about it.

Chapter 3

GRAMMAR

LANGUAGE AND GRAMMAR are expressions of a people's history, their culture and their religion. We are very often told that grammar is an artificial matter, and that it is subject to change and development, and critics of the new grammar are accused of believing that our traditional grammar is somehow a special revelation from God. It is not necessary (nor sensible) to believe that grammar is a revelation from God in order to deny the radical relativism of the new grammar. Grammar and language are indeed relative to a culture, but the fact of a degree of relativity does not make it necessary (nor sensible) to affirm a radical relativism. Neither man nor his world is absolute; they are God's creation, so that they are *first* of all relative to God, and, *second*, to the rest of creation. There is a degree of relativity in all creation. It is the humanist who seeks an absolutism in this world by asserting a radical relativity; by reducing all things around man and in man's world to flux and change, he thereby isolates man as his new absolute. The fact that language and grammar are relative to a people's faith and history does not mean that there is therefore no element of value and truth in them. Instead, we need then to say that a people's language and grammar being a product of their history and faith, the kind of religion a people have will profoundly affect in time their language and grammar. Moreover, things will have a different meaning for them because of that faith. Because of our failure to understand this, we often reinterpret the works of another culture in terms of our own world of meaning. A classic example of this is Aristotle, who would never have understood what the Scholastics and moderns are talking about when they expound Aristotelian thought. For him, words such as cause, substance, law, ethics, nature, and so on had a radically different meaning.

Another fact of importance is that language and grammar reflect the time-sense of a people, their religious faith concerning the meaning of time. Chinese civilization has a relativism of perhaps 2,000 years or more, certainly at least 1,500 years old. The result is a language without anything comparable to our grammar and time-sense. The more developed the time-sense of a people, the more simple usually is their language. Chinese and various native American Indian languages represent a wide divergence in cultural inheritance, but they have in common a high complexity. There is a subtlety of expression for the nuances of the existential moment, together with an awkwardness in dealing with the past and the future. Of the African mind (and languages), we are told, by an African philosopher, John Mbiti, that there is a lack of the category of the future as Western (Christian) thought has developed it. The African consciousness is concerned with the past, the present, and the immediate future, and whatever does not fit into these three categories is *no-time*. The linear concept of time is alien also to African thought. *Actual time* is the present and the past. If future events are a part of the constant, inevitable, and necessary rhythm of nature, they are understood, and are regarded as *potential time*. Tomorrow thus is only that which occurred yesterday and today, on the whole. This idea of time is also common to much of the ancient world, Asia, and the modern man as it is now manifesting itself.[1]

Let us illustrate this time difference by citing two very similar statements with very different meanings. According to Plutarch, the temple of Isis at Sais had this inscription: "I am all that has come into being, and that which is, and that which shall be; and no man hath lifted my veil." Contrast this with the declaration of our Lord: "I am Alpha and Omega, the beginning and the ending, saith the Lord, which is, and which was, and which is to come, the Almighty" (Rev. 1:8). Isis declares herself to be process, the procession of time and being. Everything has come into being out of her and is identical with her, a pantheistic concept. She herself is past and present and all that was and is. There is, however, no knowledge of the future: it is veiled and beyond knowing. Isis (of tomorrow) neither sees nor is seen. Thus, we have here a world of chance, not of predestination.

---

1. See Peter Berger, Brigitte Berger, Hansfried Kellner, *The Homeless Mind: Modernization and Consciousness* (New York, N.Y.: Random House, 1973), pp. 149–151.

By contrast, Jesus Christ, the Almighty God, declares Himself to be the Eternal One who is the Creator of all things and the only source of the meaning of all things, their Alpha and Omega. Moreover, He is the absolute predestinator of all things and shall appear or come as their judge.

The two "similar" statements are thus a world apart. Christ's statement has reshaped Western languages and grammars, and, through Bible translation, is reshaping the languages of peoples all over the world. Bible translating is an exacting task, because it involves in effect the reworking of a language in order to make it carry the meaning of the Bible. This means a new view of the world, of God, time, and language. I was told once by a missionary that a native convert, having now a Wycliffe Bible translation of portions of Scripture, declared, "We speak a new tongue now."

All our Western languages manifest clearly the marks of Biblical faith and translation. They have been made more and more relative to Biblical categories of thought and meaning. Our ideas of grammar, of tense, syntax, and structure, of thought and meaning, bear a Christian imprint. Very clearly, our language and grammar are relative, but relative to a heritage of Biblical faith. The new grammar is hostile to this faith and tradition: its motivation is an existential humanism. Any compromise with it involves a radical surrender of much more than language forms.

Chapter 4

TEACHING COMPOSITION

TEACHING COMPOSITION MEANS, *first*, teaching *good writing*. Its purpose is not to produce professional writers but to enable every person to write clearly and intelligibly. *Second*, good writing is *clear thinking*. Muddled thinking and writing is a headache in every area of life. The Christian school in particular should be most productive of good writing and clear thinking if it is intelligently faithful to its Biblical foundations. *Third*, the purpose of punctuation and good grammar is to *further clear thinking*, and hence there is a necessity for an increased emphasis here.

Thought without words is impossible for man. Thought implies structure, order, and words. Words give expression to ideas, abstractions, collective things and constituent aspects, so that *thinking is a verbal skill*. Grammar, then, gives structure, intelligent sequence, and temporal order to word arrangements. The word "grammar" comes from the Greek *graphein* to write. Thought means words, and words mean ideas, structure. One of the names of Jesus Christ is the Word or Logos, meaning the structure or word of life. The Arian idea of a wordless God was in actuality an affirmation of the death of God, as I point out in *The Foundations of Social Order*.

Many today oppose the idea of propositional truth. Truth cannot be reduced to propositions, they claim, so that all creedal statements are invalid. To deny propositional truth is to deny all truth and to affirm a meaningless universe in which blind forces hint at but never attain any meaning. As Christians, we must affirm not only propositional truth, but that words are miniature propositional truths. Words are aspects of a reality and a means of assessing, weighing, and measuring truth.

It should not surprise us that a humanistic era not only denies God but affirms the relativity of all things other than man, its only truth. For us, however, thinking is revelational of God, who made us in His image.

Thinking proceeds from thought, and knowledge is born from knowledge. We cannot explain the taste of strawberries to a man who has never tasted them. We can understand the nature of all reality, because the God who made us made all things else, and the knowledge of Him, and through Him of all things, is written in our being. St. Paul says that God justly condemns *all* men, whether or not they have heard the gospel,

> Because that which may be known of God is manifest in them; for God hath shewed it unto them. For the invisible things of him from the creation of the world are clearly seen, being understood by the things that are made, even his eternal power and Godhead; so that they are without excuse. (Rom. 1:19–20)

If we deny meaning, truth, propositional truth, at any one point in the universe, we then deny it at all, and we deny God as Creator. Language is not only basic to our creation as God's image-bearers, but as the medium of God's revealed Word to us. Language is thus very important in the sight of God. Hence, the abuse of language to blaspheme rather than to serve the Lord is a very serious offense. To abuse language is to mistrust an instrument given by God, used by Him to communicate with us to reveal Himself, and ordained to be our most conspicuous and central aspect in the growth and development of a godly culture.

Language is thus important, and grammar and composition are basic to the teaching of language. The teaching of language, far more than the teaching of logic, is the teaching of sound and logical thinking.

A paragraph is a body of thought: its structure is a unity in terms of an idea, concept, or datum. The paragraph must be logical and consistent. It cannot be a false syllogism. A false syllogism is a product of careless thinking rather than deliberately false thinking. The following is a false syllogism:

Man is a two-legged animal.
A chicken is a two-legged animal.
Therefore, a chicken is a man.

This illustration tells us something about a false line of thinking: it begins with a limited and faulty premise. The modern evolutionary perspective, on man and all things else, gives thinkers a false premise. In our conclusion, the statement, "Therefore, a chicken is a man," is obviously wrong. But most false syllogisms are not so clearly obvious. The thinking of modern man, resting as it does on man-centered premises, consistently winds up with erroneous if sophisticated conclusions. Our thinking must begin with God-centered premises and procedures in order to gain a sound conclusion. In all sound thinking, there are sound premises.

Marcel Duchamp, earlier in this century, attempted to create a language which would dispense with God and meaning, with propositional truth, and finally abandoned the effort as impossible. Any sound view of language and writing must rest on the premises Duchamp sought to eliminate.

Thought must precede *writing*. Thus, compositions dealing with ideas are far more useful than, "What I Did on My Vacation." It is far better to deal with, "Why Capital Punishment?" and "Should Schools Have Corporal Punishment?"

Copying is good discipline. Students who go to reference books and copy, somewhat altered, materials therefrom, are usually the better students. Condensing encyclopedia articles is good training. It requires getting to the heart of a matter, seeing essentials, and tracing the basic sequence of thought. The teacher can copy magazine and encyclopedia articles and ask all the students to condense the article as a good writing exercise.

Oral composition is excellent training. Talking is composition. I am a writer; my talks are compositions. I was trained in both oral and written composition and profited from it. Oral composition requires us to face the results of our thinking in their audience impact. Its style is different from a writing style, but the necessary ingredients are the same: having something to say, and saying it clearly and ably.

Students can be asked to give "How to" talks on their interests, how to bake bread, solder, etc. "How to" writing is also good.

Sentence structure is important. *Outlining* an essay, locating topic sentences, parsing, etc., all need to be taught.

Biblical exegesis is excellent training in good thinking and writing. A proverb from Scripture, such as Proverbs 13:24, and 28:4, 9, can be used as the first sentence of an essay to develop and explain its meaning.

The study of words is important so that they can be used precisely. An unforgettable episode in my own learning, as a university senior, was when I once used the word *raised* in an essay, and spoke of myself as having been *raised*. Professor G. Dundas Craig, an excellent teacher of composition, smiled and said, "Mr. Rushdoony, children are *reared*, and pigs are *raised*."

Children should be assigned words to look up and write about their history and meaning using the second, unabridged edition of Webster's *Dictionary*, or the *Oxford English Dictionary*.

The goal is not *creative* writing but *good* writing.

Chapter 5

MATHEMATICS

IN THE FIRST issue of the *Journal of Christian Reconstruction*, published by Chalcedon, an article by Vern S. Poythress dealt with the theological foundations of mathematics, a subject treated in greater depth later in *The Foundations of Christian Scholarship*.[1] It was quickly apparent to me how important these articles are. Not only were some graduate students awaiting their publication eagerly, but others were attacking them without seeing them. I referred to the two articles briefly, suggesting them to those interested in mathematics, when lecturing at a fundamentalist college. The professor of mathematics, without any more knowledge of those articles than my passing reference, spent the rest of the day in an emotional attack against any such premise as the two titles suggested. After the evening meeting, two students, girls, were so hysterical and rude in attacking me verbally in the hallway, in the light of the mathematics' professor's comments, that an embarrassed department head decided that some kind of discipline would be taken.

Why should so apparently routine a subject as mathematics create so savage a response again and again? Why should such titles, as "Creation and Mathematics; or, What Does God Have to Do with Numbers?" and, "A Biblical View of Mathematics," elicit so insane a response from atheists and Arminians alike?

The key to the reason why appears tellingly in an article by Danielle Hunebelle. In discussing the Belgian mathematician, Georges Papy, Hunebelle writes:

---

1. See Vern S. Poythress, "Creation and Mathematics; or, What Does God Have to Do With Numbers?" *Journal of Christian Reconstruction*, I, no. I (Summer 1974): pp. 128–140; Vern S. Poythress, "A Biblical View of Mathematics," in Gary North, ed., *The Foundations of Christian Scholarship* (Vallecito, CA: Ross House Books, 1976), pp. 159–188.

What is Papy doing? He is trying to create elementary mathematics in harmony with modern mathematics based on sets. For example, he tells beginners, "You are going to create a set." Then the child will suggest some kind of odd set: a teacher, a pickle, and a pinch of salt. "Now look how important my decision is," Papy told me. "I call this set S. It now exists because I have created it. In old mathematics, you contemplated a pre-established world. Today it is *I*, it is the child, who creates this world, who makes decisions, and who is aware of the fact that he is deciding."[2]

It is interesting to note that Papy has taught his modern mathematics to about a third of all Belgian mathematics teachers, and half of the participating teachers come from church-run schools.

One of the problems in any discussion of this subject is that, invariably, a side issue is made central, i.e., this or that aspect of modern mathematics has clarified certain aspects of our thinking or science, or contributed to a better organization of mathematical knowledge, and so on. The key issue, which Papy and Hunebelle set forth, is evaded: is there a pre-established world, or does the mind of man create a world out of chaos?

Before turning to that question, let us examine briefly the very important chapter in Spengler's study of civilization entitled, "The Meaning of Numbers." Spengler pointed out that each culture has its own concept of numbers and mathematics. Despite the adulation of the ancient Greeks, our culture, Spengler held, is radically different. Greek humanism was hostile to the idea of infinity, in mathematics, science, and religion, whereas modern humanism ascribes infinity to the universe. There is no such thing, according to Spengler, as mathematic, only mathematics. Each culture creates its own idea of numbers and sees reality in terms of it.

Every philosophy has hitherto grown up in conjunction with a mathematic *belonging* to it. Number is the symbol of causal necessity. Like the conception of God, it contains the ultimate meaning of the world-as-nature. The existence of numbers may therefore be called a mystery, and the religious thought of every Culture has felt their impress.[3]

2. Danielle Hunebelle, "Turning the Tables on Arithmetic," *Realities*, no. 157 (December, 1963): p. 42.

3. Oswald Spengler, *The Decline of the West*, vol. 1 (New York, N.Y.: Alfred A. Knopf, [1926] 1944), p. 56.

Up to a point, Spengler is right. Various religions do create their cultures and their mathematics. This is a fact almost as obvious as the existence of different languages, peoples, and races. A culture is a unity: every aspect manifests a common character. However, to point this out begs the question. To say that there are many religions does not answer the question, is there a true religion? To say that there are many mathematics does not therefore mean that there is no mathematic. Spengler, Hunebelle, Papy, Patrick Suppes, and others all begin with an essential humanism. It is religiously essential for them that man create his own world and hence his own mathematics. Because for them there is no God, there can be no mathematic, only various man-created mathematics. Man no more approaches the sciences and mathematics with neutrality than he does God, the Bible, and theology. He comes to mathematics as a covenant-keeper or a covenant-breaker with God. There is thus no area of science which constitutes common ground on which all faiths can agree. Poythress has stated the case very clearly:

> It may surprise the reader to learn that not *everyone* agrees that "2 + 2 = 4" is true. But, on second thought, it must be apparent that no radical monist can remain satisfied with "2 + 2 = 4." If with Parmenides one thinks that all is one, if with Vedantic Hinduism he thinks that all plurality is illusion, "2 + 2 = 4" is an illusory statement. On the ultimate level of being, 1 + 1 = 1.
>
> What does this imply? Even the simplest arithmetical truths can be sustained only in a worldview which acknowledges an ultimate metaphysical plurality in the world — whether Trinitarian, Polytheistic, or chance-produced plurality. At the same time, the simplest arithmetical truths also presuppose ultimate metaphysical *unity* for the world — at least sufficient unity to guard the continued existence of "sames." Two apples *remain* two apples while I am counting them; the symbol "2" is in some sense the *same* symbol at different times, standing for the *same* number.
>
> So, at the very beginning of arithmetic, we are already plunged into the metaphysical problem of unity and plurality, of the one and the many. As Van Til and Rushdoony have pointed out, this problem finds its solution only in the doctrine of the ontological Trinity. For the moment, we shall not dwell on the thorny metaphysical arguments, but note only that without *some* real unity and plurality, "2 + 2 = 4" falls into limbo. The "agreement" over mathematical truth is achieved partly by the process, described

so elegantly by Thomas Kuhn and Michael Polanyi, of excluding from the scientific community people of differing convictions.[4]

As Poythress points out, and his analysis deserves very careful study, the Christian metaphysics of mathematics is founded in the being of the triune God.[5]

For the Christian, mathematics is not the means of denying the idea of God's pre-established world in order to play god and create our own cosmos, but rather is a means whereby we can think God's thoughts after Him. It is a means towards furthering our knowledge of God's creation and towards establishing our dominion over it under God.

The issue in mathematics today is root and branch a religious one.

---

4. Poythress, "Biblical View of Mathematics," p. 161.
5. ibid., p. 176ff.

Chapter 6

TEACHING CIVICS, GOVERNMENT
& CONSTITUTION

ONE OF THE basic requirements in most states, in some instances the only requirement made for Christian schools, is a course on government and constitution. This, the older civics course, now has a variety of modern names. In each case, the training called for is a course of study in civil government.

The Christian school does not need a state requirement to be concerned about this matter: it is basic to Christian faith. *First* and foremost, our God is king over all creation, and He declares of Christ that "the government shall be upon his shoulder," and, "Of the increase of his government and peace there shall be no end" (Isa. 9:6–7). For us, government is thus not simply a *political* concern but a *theological* matter. Our obedience is more than merely a routine matter: it is for us a question of conscience. For us, civil authorities are called to be ministers of God, a holy diaconate (Rom. 13:1–8). A faithless ministry in the state is as important a concern to us, or should be, as a faithless ministry in the church. No state and no man can be neutral to the Lord. To neglect Jesus Christ is to deny His sovereign claims. Every civil order is an establishment of religion.

This means, *second*, that education for citizenship is very important to us, because our citizenship must be a part of our life in Christ and our citizenship in the Kingdom of God. Fallen man has lived both at ease and in rebellion with every type of civil government. His criterion in judging a civil order is personal and egocentric: what does it do for me? For the Christian, the criterion must be the Lord. Is this civil order faithful and obedient to Christ the King?

One of the greatest heresies of the modern era is the belief in neutrality.

Man, it is held, can be neutral about some or all things. Practically, this means that man can step outside of God's government in these neutral areas and play god on his own.

At different times, different areas of neutrality have been claimed. Many declare the state to be a neutral area. Many more hold that schools can be neutral. Still others now insist that sexuality is a neutral area and hence amoral. These claims to neutrality assert (a) the possibility and necessity for neutrality in these areas and others, and (b) the *superiority* of the supposedly neutral as against the Christian. We are told that the actually humanistic schools are neutral, and that they are therefore supposedly superior. For us, as Christians, there are no neutral areas. God is Lord over all things, and all things must serve and obey Him. Homosexuality, theft, murder, false witness, and the dishonoring of parents are sins wherever they occur. They are not made righteous or permissible by a different setting.

The Christian school is an anti-neutralist institution. It must teach that Christ is Lord over all things, including the state, and that God's law is binding on all men and nations, because He is the Lord of all. Noah Webster began his textbook, *History of the United States* (1832), with a survey of the book of Genesis, and he concluded with a chapter, "Advice to the Young," calling for godliness in Christ as the hope of the United States. Webster recognized that neither history nor life can be lived apart from a religious and moral faith, and hence he made no attempt to be "neutral." The modern pretense to scholarly neutrality is a fraud by means of which a humanistic religion is propagated as the supposedly objective and neutral reality of things. Such an approach is alien to our faith, and destructive of the Christian school. To illustrate Webster's approach, in his chapter on "Bills of Credit," or paper money, he made these "general remarks on bills of credit":

> All the colonies sooner or later issued bills of credit to supply the place of specie, which was scarce and not sufficient for a currency medium. In those colonies where the paper was immediately called in by taxes and duties, it depreciated but little; in others, it sunk to a low value, and gave debtors an opportunity to defraud their creditors, by paying them in a depreciated currency. As the paper could not circulate in foreign countries, it would not

answer for a remittance for goods imported; merchants of course preferred specie to paper, and silver rose in value. In short, a paper currency while the country was rapidly settling, and its trade restricted, was very useful in many respects; but it also produced great evils. It gave rise to unceasing jealousy and contentions between the royal and proprietary governors and the assemblies of the colonies; for the governors strenuously opposed the issuing of paper. Had the colonies been indulged in a free trade, they would have had gold and silver enough; but an unrestrained commerce could not be enjoyed, until the colonies became independent.[1]

Thus, as we have seen, the teaching of civil government is a theological concern, and it cannot be neutral. It must be Biblical; it must be Christian.

Third, it must be seen as a necessary area for godly dominion (Gen. 1:26–28; Matt. 28:18–20). We neither learn nor teach facts for their own sake, but all things for the Lord's sake. The growing failure of statist education is due to its humanism. If the state is the focus in education, as it is in "public" or state schools, then things only have meaning insofar as we choose to serve the state. The modern student, however, is increasingly anarchistic; the service of society and the state mean less and less to him. Whatever fails to please him is of no interest to him. As a result, *the content* of humanistic education declines to the degree that its humanism becomes more and more explicit.

The whole point of Christian education is that it denies the primacy of the subject. Its law is, "But seek ye first the kingdom of God, and his righteousness" (Matt. 6:33). The student in a Christian school is not there to be entertained, to "find" himself, realize himself, or advance himself, but to know, believe in, obey, and better serve the Lord, and to be prepared for his calling in the Lord. As the Lord has dominion over him, so he can have dominion in his calling through Christ.

Christian education thus prepares youths to be priests, prophets, and kings in Christ over the world. The prophetic task is to apply God's Word to our place in life, our calling, ourselves, and our families, to declare and apply God's Word. The priestly task is to dedicate ourselves, our calling, homes, and tasks to the Lord and His purposes. Our kingly task is to

---

1. Noah Webster, *History of the United States* (New Haven, CT: Durrie & Peck, 1832), p. 181.

rule ourselves, our homes, callings, and jurisdictions in Christ, to exercise dominion in all these areas in the name of the Lord and by means of His law-word.

No other agency has as important a role to play in this threefold calling of the Christian man as does the Christian school. The Christian school is more than the left hand of Christian action: it is the body thereof, and its mind.

In the teaching of government, some basic aspects of this come to focus.

Chapter 7

SCIENCE

IN THE MODERN world, science is an important part of the school curriculum for two reasons. *First*, the various sciences include *some* which have made a major impact on the modern world, and *second*, modern man tends now to believe that science, rather than Scripture, is the primary source of truth. It is important, therefore, for us to examine each of these two things carefully, if briefly.

Sciences have made, in varying degrees, a major impact on our world today, but the nature of that impact varies from one science to another. Thus, *first*, we have the very extensive impact of evolutionary theory on the modern world. The theory of evolution is not itself a science, but a theory held by many scientists in the face of facts to the contrary. The whole field of evolutionary theory, whether stemming from biology, geology, paleontology, astrophysics, or any other discipline, is important because its *religious* premises govern modern life. The world and life view of modern man is governed by evolution, and evolution is equated with science. A Christian thus must separate in his thinking and teaching the sciences from this doctrine of evolution. This does *not* mean that he can confine himself to the facts as such. There are no non-interpreted facts. In every area of life and thought, *all facts* derive their meaning from the religious presuppositions of man. These presuppositions determine what is a fact and what the interpretation of that fact shall be. Clearly, there is a world of difference between the view of an atheist and that of an orthodox Christian as they view the world. For the one, all facts are brute facts, the products of chance; for the other, all facts are God-created and therefore coherent parts of a coherent whole. Every man views factuality in terms of his basic religious premises. Thus, we do *not* replace evolution with *facts as such* but with creationism, facts as created by the sovereign and ontological Trinity.

Second, some sciences have indeed had a major impact on modern life, not in their theoretical aspects, but in their practical effects. Thus, chemistry has profoundly altered our world. The role of the chemist in the development of technology is too seldom recognized. The automotive age depends on the chemist's work, which made use of oil possible in a variety of forms. Our modern technology is heavily dependent on research scientists.

Third, it is important to avoid confusing academic scientists with research scientists. Educators tend to exalt other educators, and professors of the sciences tend to equate scientific knowledge and greatness with the university and its sciences. Our history and science textbooks are radically erroneous in their emphasis because of this prejudice, and the major part of the history of the sciences is thus unknown. With a few exceptions, the great advances in the sciences have come in association with industry, and the research scientists associated with the various corporations are basic to the modern world. This is not only true with respect to technology but also with respect to plants, trees, and the like. Take away the industrial contributions to the sciences, and we would be back in the horse and buggy age, or much further back, perhaps before the bow and arrow! To exalt academic science is to miss the point entirely and means in essence to reject science for talk about science.

Fourth, there is still another important factor, the inventor, who is not even a research scientist. It was, after all, a Kingsburg, California, barber who invented a new disc which added substantially to agricultural progress in subsequent years. Edison was an inventor, not a scientist, and many of our basic tools are the works of nonscientific men who turned inventor.

Turning now, to the other important facet of teaching science, we must remember that modern man falsely regards science rather than Scripture as the primary source of truth. *First*, we are told that science gives us verifiable truth by means of the experimental method. If science is the experimental method, then many modern sciences must be ruled unscientific, i.e., geology, astronomy, and much more. The sciences are not defined by a uniform method but by a common interest in knowledge of the physical universe. The experimental method is one means of gaining knowledge

among others. It is not an infallible method, because it is never comprehensive or total in its control of all factors; moreover, an experiment rests
on certain interpretations and hypotheses and requires others to deal with
the results.

Second, we are told that, because the sciences are concerned with the
physical world, they are concerned with reality, it being implied that
Christianity is not concerned with reality but with vague spiritual assumptions. However, as Van Til has pointed out,

> We should accordingly avoid the error of separating too sharply between
> science and religion as is often done. The world of natural and historical fact
> with which science deals cannot be truly interpreted by anyone who is not a
> Christian, any more than can the world of spiritual things. Every statement
> about the physical universe implies, in the last analysis, some view about the
> "spiritual" realm. Scientists frequently say that in their statements they will
> limit themselves to the phenomenal world. But every assertion they make
> about the "phenomenal" world involves an attitude toward the "noumenal"
> world. Even the mere assumption that anything can intelligently be asserted
> about the phenomenal world by itself presupposes its independence of God,
> and as such is in effect a denial of him.[1]

Moreover, the methodology of science involves ruling out *mind* in favor
of *matter*. Whereas the Greeks viewed reality as two alien substances, the
common popular conclusion of many scientists is that we have a single
substance, *matter*, or the physical universe, whether it be viewed as atoms
or energy. The Biblical view is against both these perspectives. The whole
of the physical universe, inclusive of "mind" and "matter," is created being, the handiwork of the sovereign God, who is uncreated being.

Thus, the truth about our physical universe is neither its duality nor its
singleness but rather its createdness, in all its rich variety. It is the work of
the sovereign and Almighty God.

The Greek attempt to reduce reality to form and matter was seriously
in error, as is the modern view. Both are reductionist and distort reality
and the sciences.

---

1. Cornelius Van Til, *An Introduction to Systematic Theology* (Nutley, NJ: Presbyterian
& Reformed Publishing Co., 1976), p. 113.

The teaching of the sciences thus must be Biblically and theologically governed. No truth nor any fact exists apart from the triune God. We cannot omit theology from the teaching of any science. The question, rather, is which theology? The theology of humanism, or the theology of Scripture? The science teachers in our humanistic state schools are consistent theologians: they teach the sovereignty of the creature and the autonomy of the mind of man as they teach every subject. The Christian teacher must be even more consistent in his faith.

Chapter 8

SCIENCE & FREEDOM

MODERN SCIENTISTS HAVE a public image of prim and proper tech-
nicians, working earnestly in scientific experimentation, and somewhat
divorced from the everyday world of human affairs. However, whatever
scientists are in person, we must say that their thinking and their sciences
are to a large degree responsible for the forms that modern revolutionary
thought has taken. More specifically, we can say that beatniks, hippies,
revolutionists, "drug-culture" peoples, and others manifest very plainly
the influence of the modern sciences.

To understand why this is so, let us note what Cornelius Van Til has
said of the goal of modern culture:

> In particular the goal of modern culture is the cultivation of self-sufficient
> free human personality. It is assumed by those who hold this ideal that the
> world of space and time is controlled by impersonal laws and that human
> freedom must be attained by setting it negatively over against the impersonal
> laws of space and time. The world of space and time is not thought of as
> embodying the laws of the creator. Therefore the idea of freedom is freedom
> that is set over against mechanism; not freedom that is found in obedience to
> God. So the goal of freedom is one of pure negation, or if it is one of affirma-
> tion then it is that of an ideal cast up into the limitless sky of the unknown.
> Here too it is the first duty of Christians to call men to repentance lest they
> and their culture lose all meaning and men remain under the wrath of God.[1]

The dialectic of modern thought is a nature-freedom faith. The world
of nature is the world of necessity, a mechanistic realm for many, and
for all who share in the modern faith, a cold, dead realm of unthinking

---

1. Cornelius Van Til, *Essays on Christian Education* (Nutley, NJ: Presbyterian & Reformed Publishing Co., [1971] 1974), p. 5.

inevitability. Man is an evolutionary product of that kingdom of necessity. His mind is governed, formed, and determined by that realm. All the same, in his mind, man can conceive of freedom, and, like the Marxist, dream of delivering man from the kingdom of necessity to the kingdom of freedom.

Marxism is one of several faiths which have attempted to work that deliverance. The unhappy fact is that there is no valid reason for calling the attempts anything other than predetermined responses governed and created by the kingdom of necessity. As a result, when nature is necessity, it follows that freedom is impotent to do more than negate. *Negation* has thus become important to modern man, senseless negation. We have the senseless crime, the irrational behavior of rebels without a cause, and the delight in perversity deeply imbedded in the modern character.

Thus, Apollinaire advocated, in the 1885–1914 era, *the gratuitous act* as the expression of human freedom. "One can maintain that the only domain of purely disinterested action that remains is the inversion of charity: *unmotivated evil.* It satisfies nothing deeper than whim."[2] This type of behavior has become routine since then among modern youth. Nature is the realm of necessity and law, and *hence freedom means lawlessness.*

For us, however, as Van Til states, freedom "is found in obedience to God," and God is the source and author of the universe and of all law. Thus, neither nature, i.e., the physical universe, nor law are hostile to freedom but rather basic to it.

It is basic to any teaching of science in a Christian school, therefore, that the idea of an impersonal realm of law and matter be discarded. The end result of any such teaching will be a reproduction of the modern mentality.

Moreover, such a view of the physical universe as a realm of impersonal action and law is alien to Scripture and hostile to it. We dare not destroy the meaning of, for example, Nahum 1:2–8, by reducing it to poetry. Nahum describes as literal fact God's totally personal control and use of the physical universe towards His sovereign purposes. The natural and supernatural realms are set forth as totally governed and used by the Lord

---

2. Roger Shattuck, *The Banquet Years* (Garden City, NY: Doubleday Anchor Books, [1955] 1961), p. 304.

for His purposes, and for none other. Nothing in God's creation has a life of its own. Nahum thus declares:

> God is jealous, and the LORD revengeth: the LORD revengeth, and is furious; the LORD will take vengeance on his adversaries, and he reserveth wrath for his enemies. The LORD is slow to anger, and great in power, and will not at all acquit the wicked; the LORD hath his way in the whirlwind and in the storm, and the clouds are the dust of his feet. He rebuketh the sea, and maketh it dry, and drieth up all the rivers: Bashan languisheth, and Carmel, and the flower of Lebanon languisheth. The mountains quake at him, and the hills melt, and the earth is burned at his presence, yea, the world, and all that dwell therein. Who can stand before his indignation? and who can abide in the fierceness of his anger? his fury is poured out like fire, and the rocks are thrown down by him. The LORD is good, a strong hold in the day of trouble; and he knoweth them that trust in him. But with an overrunning flood he will make an utter end of the place thereof, and darkness shall pursue his enemies. (Nahum 1:2–8)

Only such a faith can preserve science. The naturalistic view not only produces a view of freedom as negation, but also a view of nature as mindless and therefore meaningless. Science cannot long continue when the physical universe becomes a world of brute, meaningless factuality, and man's only hope, then, is in freedom as the gratuitous act of negation.

Moreover, the modern view of science leads to a deadly reductionism. Reality is reduced to matter, and, as a result, the whole world of Scripture is seen as nonessential and peripheral at best. Man is seen as not truly alive unless he is experienced in the physical realm. As a result, sexuality, travel, and physical experiences of various kinds assume religious dimensions. Religion is, as Tillich saw, ultimate concern. If our ultimate concern is with physical reality, then sex will become a necessary religious experience which we cannot live without. We will be ready to believe also that a man has not really lived unless he has travelled to this or that place, undergone various physical sensations, and so on.

Science teaching which gives us the world of Einstein and Bohr will simply predispose the student towards the popular religious cult of the physical. If our science teaching is not in terms of the world Nahum and all of Scripture sets forth, we will soon lose our students to a rival faith, and science to meaninglessness. The universe of modern science is empty of meaning; such a view is productive of empty lives, men possessed by a sense of overwhelming meaninglessness, a sense of chaos and the void. A faith which sees every fact in the universe as a personal fact and as the creation of the totally personal and sovereign God will provide man with meaning and growth and power in terms of God's universe of meaning.

Chapter 9

TEACHING SCIENCE

SCIENCE TEACHING IS made more than normally important because science in the modern world has for many replaced God as the source of authority. In one field after another, appeal is made to the authority of science; in politics, where we have scientific socialism; in religion, in the forms of modernism; in education, in progressivist theory; and so on. If we fail to teach science properly, we will only enhance its false authority and obscure its use.

For a Christian, the task of *instruction* is made simpler by the fact that the Biblical, Hebrew word for instruction, Torah, means both *law* and *instruction*. For us, all things in every sphere are under an ultimate and fundamental law, God's law, and education is instruction in that law order. Modern science is a product of a Biblical worldview, with its belief in God and the world under God's law. Without that substructure, science will quickly disintegrate.

Thus, for the science teacher, the ultimacy of God must be basic. For the humanist, it is the ultimacy of this world which is basic. Scientifically, the consequences of our faith are very great for the doctrine of causality alone. In the Biblical faith, we have a marked difference in being between the uncreated Being of God and the created being of the universe. This difference makes possible the distinction between the ultimate and primary cause, God, and all secondary causes within creation. Where the Creator-creature distinction is blurred or denied, secondary causes disappear, and pantheism, a single cause, emerges. Some churchmen who have thought to honor God by denying secondary causes have regularly ended by destroying the faith and by negating the doctrine of creation.

Humanistic science, by positing as an article of faith the ultimacy of the universe, has as a result a strong tendency towards determinism and the denial of secondary causes as anything more than an illusion. Man is a product of the universe and is totally conditioned thereby. The result is the death of responsibility. The only way humanism has out of this trap is to affirm no universe at all, but only brute factuality and radical anarchy, or total indeterminism. Biblical faith alone preserves the integrity of the ultimate cause, and the reality of secondary causes. Man's responsibility is real, because creation is real, is separate from God's being but not government, and is not an illusion, nor merely an aspect of ultimate being.

It should not surprise us therefore that modern science was not only born out of Christianity, but especially out of a Puritan context in seventeenth-century England. This Christian orientation persisted almost into the twentieth century. Popular history to the contrary, science did not find its origins in the thought of men like Giordano Bruno. Bruno's humanism led him rather into occultism.[1] In a universe without God, either blind fate renders man meaningless, or a chaotic universe gives man the opportunity to be an occult lord. Not dominion but power becomes man's goal.

Among the early Puritan leaders in the sciences, a postmillennial perspective was prominent in their minds. Science was a means of exercising dominion. Significantly, even nonorthodox scientists shared a strong interest in eschatology. Thus, Isaac Newton, while having Unitarian or Socinian ideas about Jesus Christ, still spent time and study in writing about *Revelation*. Scientists were concerned, because science was seen as a means of fulfilling God's command to exercise dominion and to subdue the earth.

The Christian and the non-Christian approach the universe differently and hence define it differently. The humanist, because this world is all, is confident in definition. *Life*, for example, is defined chemically and physiologically, within totally naturalistic confines. If the reality of our world is entirely natural, then definition is relatively easy. Given enough time, all things can be defined after sufficient research, dissection, experimentation, or study. From a Christian perspective, this is not true. Leviticus 17:11 makes it clear that life is "in the blood," but it is even more clear that

---

1. See Frances A. Yates, *Giordano Bruno and the Hermetic Tradition* (New York, NY: Random House, Vintage Books, [1964] 1969).

life is not *from* the blood but from God (Gen. 2:7). To understand life, we must look *beyond* life to God. Definition is more than naturalistic: it goes beyond us and our world, and is thus in essence impossible. For us, therefore, science is not definitive but *descriptive and theological.* Science becomes more productive as it abandons its goal to define naturalistically, which leads to theoretical science, and limits itself to description in terms of theological premises.

The theological foundation also means a realistic view of scientific goals. Because God is God, this means simply that "with God all things are possible" (Matt. 19:26). If the physical universe is ultimate, then it follows logically that, with nature, all things are possible. Because humanistic scientists operate on this premise of the ultimacy of nature and its infinite potentiality, they are ever ready to experiment or to hypothesize in areas known to be impossible from scientific experience. Thus, science tells us that spontaneous generation is not possible, and yet it is a necessary postulate in evolutionary thought. Because infinite potentiality is ascribed, not to God but to nature, this impossibility is only impossible in the present; in infinite time, the infinite potentiality of nature overcomes all limitations.

Current genetic research also operates in terms of infinite potentiality. Organ transplants are clear examples of this. The June 1977 attempt to transplant a baboon's heart into a human being failed; it was done in the clear knowledge that transplants face a rejection factor: they are like an alien and infecting agent to the host body. The hope is, however, that man can overcome this barrier, and the hope rests on the faith that infinite potentiality belongs to nature rather than to God. The same is true of hybridization; all hybrids are sterile, but the hope continues that a mule will someday be fertile.

Thus, the lines God created between various forms of life and inorganic matter are seen as enemies by humanistic science, because this fixity denies the infinite potentiality of nature. But this is not all. Because eternity is an attribute of ultimacy, time is a problem to the humanist, and an enemy. Hence the hostility to clock time.[2]

---

2. See R. J. Rushdoony, *The Mythology of Science* (Nutley, NJ: The Craig Press, [1967] 1976), pp. 76–77.

Because for humanistic science all potentiality belongs to nature, it is easy for scientists to read their beliefs in infinite possibility into their research. The result is a massive trend to scientific fraud in experimentation. This is not new, as witness the drawings of the development of the human embryo by Haeckel in the last century. *Science Digest* (June 1977) has called attention to the high percentage of frauds in reported scientific experiments. The attitude of such researchers apparently is that, "if it isn't true now, it soon will be."

One of the major problems in all teaching, and no less in the teaching of science, is the dominance of an academic orientation. For example, biology, chemistry, and physics are taught in isolation from one another, as though a different world existed for each. This means that an abstracted and academic view of science prevails, with theoretical science predominant. If we teach instead the history of scientific research, development, and invention, and the role of the various areas in that history of development and application, we gain a more accurate knowledge of the place of science and its meaning. From such an approach, we gain a more realistic view of the sciences and how man has tried to understand himself and the world through science, and to exercise dominion through that knowledge and by means of the instruments it has produced.

The humanistic curriculum has exalted subjects and their study as an end in themselves. Art for art's sake has been paralleled by science for science's sake. Science for man's sake is no better unless we view man theologically and view science as a tool for man in his calling to exercise dominion.

Chapter 10

THE EXPERIMENTAL METHOD

THE EXPERIMENTAL METHOD has had a very great influence on popular culture. The idea of an antiseptic scientist, purged of all germs of preconceived ideas, arriving at scientific truth, has had a deep influence on the popular imagination.

Of course, if science is limited to the experimental method, then a great many of the sciences, such as geology, paleontology, botany, and more, are not scientific. As a result, it is now more common to speak of *the scientific method*, a broader and more vague term which has the aura of experimental "proof": and none of its burdens.

The scientific method is never carefully defined, but, like the term science, is somehow equated with *truth*. Thinkers in the sciences are prompt to assure us that science does not pretend to offer infallible truth. This seems the essence of modesty and a proper disclaimer, except that, having said this, they are still emphatic in holding that, whatever truth there is, if it can be known, it will be discovered and known through the scientific method. The Moslems say, there is one God, and Mohammed is his prophet. The scientists are no less dogmatic: there may or may not be truth, but if there is, science is its prophet, the only means to its discovery. Notice what George Sarton has to say: "Science . . . is the whole body of systematized and objective knowledge; it is very incomplete and very imperfect, but it is indefinitely perfectible."[1] This definition of science excludes revelation as a source of knowledge. Sarton's view of science is clearly one in which knowledge has one source and voice, one prophet, and it is science. More accurately, we should say *scientists*, because we

---

1. George Sarton, "Introductory Essay," in Joseph Needham, ed., *Science: Religion & Reality* (New York, NY: George Braziller, [1925] 1955), p. 3.

cannot abstract science from man's thinking and project it into mental space as an independent entity.

It is important for us to grasp the implications of the pretensions of the scientific method. If not, because it is so deeply imbedded in our culture and books, students will unconsciously pick up this equation of science with knowledge, a dangerous and fallacious equation.

W. F. G. Swann was emphatic that the scientist must "avoid all theological doctrine as a starting point."[2] Such men do not thereby eliminate a religious premise and starting point. Rather, they substitute for Christianity a humanistic religion as their foundation.

The premise behind this method has been ably described by Cornelius Van Til:

> In paradise Satan had won the heart of man away from God to himself. He had done so by the cleverest of strategems. He had done so by making Eve and Adam believe that while eating of the tree of knowledge of good and evil they were engaging in the first really scientific enterprise. It was an experiment far more significant in its consequences for human culture than the first trip made recently to the moon.
>
> There were two mutually opposing hypotheses with respect to the possible consequences of eating the fruit of that tree. There was the theory of the one party who called himself God and who, therefore, in dogmatic fashion, asserted that "death" would be the only possible consequence of eating of the forbidden fruit. Then there was the theory of the second party. This party was not dogmatic at all. He only claimed that scientific experimentation requires an open mind. Especially was this true, in the case of the *first* scientific experiment ever to be made. There were no records of what had happened in the past. And to speak of this tree, in distinction from all other trees, as a "forbidden" tree is to assume that one party alone owned all the world.
>
> In his "genuine freedom of choice" man must therefore decide between these two available hypotheses.[3]

---

2. W. F. G. Swann, "Yesterday, Today, and Tomorrow," in Webster P. True, ed., *Smithsonian Treasury of 20th-Century Science* (New York, NY: Simon and Schuster, 1966), p. 529. The title of this book is of interest. The use of the word "treasury" was made popular by the Victorians, but is now in common use among scientists and humanists, as they pass on their gems of wisdom to us.

3. Cornelius Van Til, *Essays on Christian Education* (Nutley, NJ: Presbyterian & Reformed Publishing Co., 1974), p. 25.

The point, I think, is clear. The scientific method, as it now exists, is in reality a religious principle which holds that truth can emerge from any area, provided it is not from the sovereign and triune God and His infallible Word. The scientific method of our time masks another religion, humanism.

The results of science today are in spite of their method. In terms of their presuppositions, the universe has no design nor order, and chance rules totally. In such a view, science and knowledge are impossible. The results obtained by science presuppose an orderly world, one with law, structure, and meaning. In other words, an atheistic world is affirmed, but, in actual research and study, a theistic world is assumed.

Thus, Mario G. Salvadori, a mathematician at Columbia University, held that,

> Mathematics is a game in which the players set up their own rules and play with no other purpose than to play according to the rules. Any player may at any time change any rule, provided this change does not lead to contradictory rules. Since, moreover, mathematics may be played by a single individual, the player doesn't even need the consent of one or more partners in order to change a rule.
>
> This definition of mathematics will come as a shock to all but the mathematical expert.[4]

Contemporary mathematicians delight in making such statements; it makes man god in a universe of his own devising. Too few will add, as Salvadori did, "That mathematics is the purest of games should not obscure the fact that most of its rules have roots in reality and were originally suggested by practical situations."[5] We have two different worlds in these two statements.

This humanistic view of science and the scientific method strips man of all meaning other than a purely material and biological one. Thus, Dr. R. W. Gerard, M.D., of the University of Michigan's Mental Health Research Institute, held that a man's morals are really accidents of his time and place in history.[6]

---

4. Mario G. Salvadori, "Mathematics, the Language of Science," in Lyman Bryson, ed., *An Outline of Man's Knowledge of the Modern World* (Garden City, NY: Nelson Doubleday, 1960), p. 193.
5. ibid., p. 194.
6. R. W. Gerard, M.D., "The Brain, Mechanism of the Mind," in ibid., pp. 73–89.

The biologist, Hudson Hoagland, held that there are

...only two answers to the question of how life began. It must either have arisen spontaneously from nonliving material or have been created by supernatural means. If one accepts the second answer, science has nothing to contribute, since the question cannot be resolved by the operational approaches of scientists.[7]

What Hoagland is saying is that, unless scientists can play god and fathom the creation of and/or reproduce life itself, there is no science, because then "science has nothing to contribute." The fact that science would then have much to understand, and to understand more coherently than at present, he refuses to consider. Basic to all humanism is the tempter's plan of Genesis 3:5, man as his own god, knowing or determining for himself what constitutes good and evil. Scientists outside of Christ prefer to think, with Dr. Meyer Maskin, M.D., of the New York University College of Medicine, who held it likely that man may "be on his way toward creating a new human species."[8]

What such ideas have done is to mold the mind of students against God and His Word. What God declares is ruled out of education as *not knowledge*. If the Bible is what it declares itself to be, then it is the most basic book in education. All knowledge must be organized in terms of the God of Scripture as the Creator and Interpreter of all reality.

Apart from that book, we have the superstitions of modern humanistic education (e.g., spontaneous generation, evolution, etc.) and a growing moral decay and social disintegration. Education declines, and barbarism sets in.

The scientific method is in essence a religious method, an atheistic, humanistic methodology. Our scientific *and* educational method must be theological. We begin with the fact of God as Creator, and the world as His handiwork. Apart from that fact, we have, not knowledge, but misinformation.

---

7. Hudson Hoagland, "The Elements of Life," in ibid., p. 151.
8. Meyer Maskin, "The Science of Personality," in ibid., p. 99.

Chapter 11

MUSIC

THE HUMANISTIC PHILOSOPHY of music is ably summarized by the state of Ohio in its *Minimum Standards* in these words:

Music, as one of the fine arts, is an integral part and an enriching force in the life of the individual. As a required part of the elementary school curriculum, the music program includes learning opportunities for children of varying levels of musical abilities and achievements (those who create, those who perform, those who enjoy and those who may become professional musicians). The instruction emphasizes the development of aesthetic sensitivity, creative capacity, cultural awareness, musical competence, and intelligence.[1]

One of the aspects of the music program is to relate "music and other human experiences."[2]

Unhappily, all too many Christians would find no fault with this statement. Their own philosophy of music is so saturated with humanism, that they find it difficult to understand why this statement is so wrong.

The focus of humanistic music is, as the *Minimum Standards* indicate, on "the life of the individual." By means of music, the individual is to find his emotional self-expression, development, and enrichment.

Music in the modern era has had this focus and concern to an increasing degree. It began very much under the influence of Christian music, so that, whether on the classical or the popular level, music, from the Enlightenment on, shows the clear but waning impact of Christian music. In the twentieth century, this influence has become more remote, and, in fact, a contrary influence began to appear, the influence of non-Christian

---

1. Virginia M. Lloyd, ed., *Minimum Standards for Ohio Elementary Schools* (Columbus, OH: State of Ohio, Department of Education, July 1970), p. 74.
2. ibid.

music on church music. This was far from new. Much earlier, operatic and romantic music had exercised its influences, but, with the twentieth century, the determination of church music by secular music became especially dominant.

Meanwhile, humanistic music had also taken two directions which reflected the schizophrenia implicit in its nature. *First,* in popular music there came in full bloom from jazz to acid rock music the concentration on the use of music to exploit feeling for the sake of feeling. Music had never been devoid of emotion, and it had always been the function of music to arouse emotions and to enhance them. This emotional function of music had always been subject, however, to a specific purpose other than feeling as such. The emotions aroused could be awe, reverence, joy, or whatever else was desired, in terms of a religious, festival, martial, marital, or other purpose. A march, as a set form, could serve a variety of purposes and emotions: it could be a wedding march, an academic procession, a church rite, a parade ground march, a war-charged march, a civil function, and so on. Now the emphasis is on feeling for its own sake. Not surprisingly, in acid rock, music is allied to a narcotic to produce an emotionalism which cuts all ties to reality to enter into "pure" emotionalism. Of course, this goal is an impossible one. The individual cannot escape from God's reality; he carries it into the drugged world of music, and hence the radical results of such music. The desire is for increased drugs and escapist music, and a wilder flight from reality. In all this, humanism's emphasis on the individual and his autonomous self and enrichment is very much in evidence.

Second, in "classical" music, a similar emphasis on the individual has been in evidence, but in a different direction. Composers have produced a rationalistic, overly intellectual music, one in which emotions are sometimes squeezed out. Experimentation is made with new scales, dissonance, and new sounds, and also with distortions.

The older music was at times program music, written to illustrate or tell something, and with a governing external factor. Abstract music, such as Bach's fugues, was not governed by a written text or an external factor, but it was still clear-cut in its expression: it followed the standards, i.e., expressing religious emotion, joy, or in some other way manifesting a unity of mind and feeling. Suggestive music, a later development, was comparable to impressionism in art: it created a mood but tied the listener less to the composer's purpose.

The new music is different. It denies the unity of mind and feeling. It strives for an autonomy from accepted and expected canons, reactions, and feelings. It seeks to communicate little other than a revolutionary sense of autonomy. Music previously could be dated. Thus, Bach, great and independent of spirit, is intensely a man of the musical past. Bach uses the musical past to express his present purposes. Bach, once appreciated, opens up a whole tradition of music to us. Similarly, Berlioz, while highly individual, is still a key figure in the culmination of certain nineteenth century musical trends, and in pointing to the twentieth century. Musicians spoke out of a tradition, a culture, a faith, and a nation, so that we can identify German, Russian, French, Italian, and American music to a considerable degree. It is this type of rooting and tradition which the new music tries to break with, although not entirely with success. It seeks an autonomy which is radical, a separation from traditional canons of music, national expression, accepted emotional patterns, and the older rational norms. Thus, we will sometimes hear, in the new music, not only a tonal dissonance, but a clash of emotional and intellectual responses, so that we cannot react as we normally do. While the results are sometimes striking and even remarkable, the overall results show a marked tendency towards impotence. Our composers too often produce musical mules.

The church has too long imitated the world in its music. The result has been, on the one hand, cheap emotional gospel music, and, on the other, sterile "high-brow" music which is more often artful than art.

However, Christianity, if true to Scripture, must be the leader in music, not the follower. It must insist on its own musical canons. *First*, the Biblical faith is unique in its strong emphasis on music. An entire book of the Bible, the Psalms, is a hymn or song book. In both Old and New Testaments, believers are commanded to sing (e.g., Isa. 12:5; Eph. 5:18–19; Col. 3:16; James 5:13).

Second, the tithe includes the support of musicians as a necessary part of worship. This fact, together with the summons to sing, has given Christendom an emphasis on music not found elsewhere in the world.

Historically, one of the more potent instruments of evangelism on mission fields has been music, and some pagan faiths, such as Buddhism, are now trying to copy Christianity and to use music to hold their believers.

Third, in Scripture the function of music is not man-centered but God-centered. Man does not sing for his own self-expression, nor for his enrichment but *because* he has been enriched by the grace of God unto salvation. This is clearly stated, for example, in Psalm 30:4: "Sing unto the LORD, O ye saints of his, and give thanks at the remembrance of his holiness." The commandment is always, sing *unto the Lord*. Hence, in older churches, not only the congregation but the choir, often located in the back of the sanctuary, sang facing the altar or the pulpit, unto the Lord. The modern choir sings *to the people*, and the people sing *the hymns which please them*. The purpose of Christian music is not man's enjoyment of the song of music, but the expression of covenant man's joy in the Lord, his gratitude, thanksgiving, petition, and prayer. Only such music can be pleasing to God, because the requirement is always *to sing unto the Lord*, whether with voice or with instrument: "Sing unto the LORD with the harp; with the harp, and the voice of a psalm" (Ps. 98:5).

Fourth, the value of music in the instruction of others depends on this God-centered emphasis. St. Paul shows this aspect of music when he declares,

> Let the word of Christ dwell in you richly in all wisdom; teaching and admonishing one another in psalms and hymns and spiritual songs, singing with grace in your hearts to the Lord. (Col. 3:16)

The meaning here is that others are taught and admonished by our songs *because* those songs are sung with grace *unto the Lord*. They may enjoy our other singing more, but God's purpose is accomplished by our God-centered singing.

It follows, certainly, that Christian music which meets this requirement calls first of all for God-centered musicians, men whose life and thought is governed by the sovereignty of God and His majesty. The Westminster Shorter Catechism begins by declaring, "Man's chief end is to glorify God, and to enjoy Him forever." This is an excellent statement of the purpose of Christian music.

Chapter 12

FOREIGN LANGUAGES

THE OHIO *Minimum Standards* give us in brief a philosophy of humanism with reference to foreign language study:

Learning a foreign language at the elementary school level contributes significantly to the development of the pupil's potential talents and interests through broadening concepts of language and increasing the ability to communicate. It helps to create a better appreciation of life in other cultural and linguistic environments, enabling the learner to participate more effectively in a modern democratic society which maintains extensive political, economic, and cultural relationships with peoples of many languages and cultures.[1]

This is a good statement of the humanistic approach. The focal point is man and society. Foreign languages are set forth as advantageous from a humanistic perspective.

Foreign language study, however, has been declining in importance for some years, and the reason for it is the development of humanism into its pragmatic and existential forms. The modern humanist is not concerned with Greek humanism, nor with the Enlightenment; the newer humanism focuses on the moment, on the here and now. As a result, more and more young simply declare, "I don't *need* a foreign language." In practical modern terms, they are usually right.

How, then, shall we justify the study of foreign languages? Shall we study Latin because it is so important to the development of English? We would have to say, then, that Anglo-Saxon and Middle English are equally if not more deserving of study, while giving the nod to Latin for

---

1. Lloyd, *Minimum Standards*, p. 45.

its historical role. Shall we study French because it was for a long era the language of diplomacy and international affairs? This was even more true of Greek, especially under Byzantine rule, for at least 800 years. German is the language of scholarship, but not to the degree that English is.

A humanistic rationale for languages faces problems. *First*, the older, classical tradition held that certain foreign languages are basic to the life of culture. This rationale is not ours. *Second*, the newer humanism sees only one need, a contemporary one, and seeks justification only in terms of the present.

There is, however, a *third* factor. Humanism has stressed those languages which are basic to the history of humanism: classical Greek, Latin, French, German, and now Russian and Chinese and with some, Spanish. All these languages are a part of the mainstream of humanistic efforts and dreams. A religious thread holds them together, the humanistic faith.

As we think about foreign languages, we too must think religiously. This means, *first* of all, that for us primacy must be given to the Biblical languages, Hebrew and Greek. Early colonial education stressed these two, and able five-year-olds were not infrequently taught both. The more important point is that the Puritans were educating their children for life in a Christian commonwealth under God. They felt, accordingly, that the most basic knowledge is of the Word of God, and of every area of life viewed in terms of God's Word. The study of Scripture was thus basic to all education for all men. For those with greater aptitudes, the Biblical languages were a necessity. Classical humanism insisted on the need for Latin and classical Greek. Modern humanism tends to view foreign languages pragmatically and usually as peripheral. Christian education will see Hebrew and New Testament Greek as basic. It is worthy of note that some Christian high schools are considering instruction in them.

Second, even as Adam was called to exercise dominion and subdue the earth (Gen. 1:26–28), redeemed man is sent into all the world with the same commission under Jesus Christ (Matt. 28:18–20). This requires Christian man to acquire eminence and dominion in every realm and to be an imperialist in Christ, asserting the crown rights of Christ the King in every area, as against nationalistic or internationalistic forms of imperialism. It should not surprise us, therefore, that the study of foreign languages has never been even remotely equal to that within Christendom among non-Christian peoples. Christianity has fostered foreign language study because Christianity sees its necessary commission to *all the world*. Thus, it is not only Greek and Hebrew but all modern foreign languages which interest Christians. Christian schools, on the whole, stress foreign language study more than do the public schools. But this is not all. The most outstanding work in linguistics, unrivalled by any university or graduate school, is done by the Wycliffe Bible Translators. In no other field are Christians more clearly in the forefront than in linguistics. Christians are the only true internationalists, because their tie to other peoples is grounded in the Creator and Redeemer of all.

Third, our faith as Christians is unique in the emphasis it places on language as the vehicle and means of God's revelation, and also because it tells us of the origin of diverse languages in the curse at Babel. Over the centuries, various languages have played their part as the language of international affairs, but it must be said that nothing has done more to bring about a common language than the Bible. The Bible reshapes every language it is translated into, and it draws it closer thereby to all other languages. The present forms of the languages of Christendom owe more to the Bible than to any other single factor. Western languages, in their development, have had a theological restructuring and therefore are different from other languages on this ground alone. These languages give us as a result a familiar thought-world: we are not total strangers to them, as we would be to a language of a still unconverted people. Each language expresses a theological experience and tradition. In due time, Christian scholars will produce landmark studies in linguistics, developing precisely this aspect of language.

Part III

Chapter 1

EDUCATION & THE FALL:
UP OR DOWN?

HUMANISM IN THE modern era has had a very simple and effective plan for conquest, control of education. By taking custody of the child's mind, it has effectively determined the future for the past century and a half. It has so thoroughly dominated education that even most of its enemies are extensively conditioned by the basic doctrines of humanism.

Where education from kindergarten through college is controlled by statist humanism, most of its products regularly reflect that faith. As a result, Christian pastors and laymen who believe themselves to be militantly Reformed are often humanistic in spite of themselves. On the whole, the longer a minister is out of seminary, the more the basic pattern of his education, *humanism*, asserts itself against his rather brief training in Reformed theology.

Moreover, whereas once the Reformed faith was a total world and life view, it is now only a theology, a fact which is compelling evidence of retreat. Reformed theologians as late as Dabney were still men who saw the faith as determinative of every area of life, not merely of theology and the doctrine of the church. Now, politics, economics, science, art, and the whole range of disciplines are largely left to the humanists, modernists, neo-evangelicals, and neo-Reformed thinkers whose essential purpose is humanism in some form or another.

The key to a recovery of a reformed world and life view is Christian education, and basic to a sound doctrine of Christian education is a Biblical view of creation and the fall. I have deliberately raised a false question with respect to the fall in order to call attention to a dangerous approach to the subject. We are accustomed to thinking of the humanistic perspective in terms of evolutionary theory in its simplest forms, namely, the ascent of man from some kind of "ape" ancestry to the status of a man. The direction in such thinking is clearly "up": it is on the ascent of man. It would seem clear that an emphasis on the "downward" character of human nature would be congenial to Biblical thought. This, however, is not necessarily so. A considerable body of sophisticated modern thought posits some kind of fall for man. Its influence is apparent in neo-orthodoxy, Marxism, Freudianism, and other schools of thought, and its key word is *alienation.* Man's fall, in such thinking, is into self-consciousness, individualism, and a separate and distinct sense of identity. The result has been an alienation from the group and a loss of group identity in favor of individual identity. One ostensibly ugly consequence of the "fall" is the sense of guilt. Modern man speaks, not of sin, but of guilt, or, more accurately, *the feeling of guilt.* Man's self-consciousness and his God-consciousness have cursed him with guilt. A modern writer complains, "I feel guilty for *everything.*"[1] This same writer, a Jewess, continues,

> Why had I been cursed with such a hypertrophied superego? Was it just being Jewish? What did Moses *do* for the Jews anyway by leading them out of Egypt and giving them the concept of one God, matzoh-ball soup, and everlasting guilt? Couldn't he just have left them alone worshipping cats and bulls and falcons or living like the other primates (to whom — as my sister Randy always reminds me — they are so closely related)? Is it any *wonder* that everyone hates the Jews for giving the world guilt? Couldn't we have gotten along nicely without it? Just sloshing around in the primeval slush and worshipping dung beetles and f——— when the mood struck us?[2]

Jong, who writes with ability and ruthless honesty, has ably posed the problem others fumble with.

The problem is this: The Christian believes that man feels guilty and *is* guilty because he is fallen, because he is by nature a sinner. The humanist believes, rather, that man is fallen because he feels guilty. The solution for the existentialist humanist is to eliminate the sense of guilt and the fall will be eliminated. For the Marxist, the solution is to eliminate

1. Erica Jong, *Fear of Flying* (New York, NY: Signet Books, [1973] 1974), p. 131.
2. ibid., p. 245.

self-consciousness and the private personality, and the fall or alienation will be eliminated. For psychoanalysts and many psychiatrists, man's problem is the feeling of guilt, and salvation is to live beyond guilt, beyond the knowledge of good and evil, beyond all religious and moral training. For modern pornography, man's problem again is the feeling of guilt, and liberation or salvation is to live without guilt.[3]

Such thinking is increasingly basic to humanism, and has been since Nietzsche and Freud. For education, it means that the fall of man is essentially Biblical religion, which must be eradicated, and whose influence must be overcome, in order to deliver man into paradise regained. All too many churchmen view the undisciplined and amoral products of statist education as evidences of the failures of these schools. On the contrary, they are evidences of their success. It is the Biblical doctrine of the fall which requires regeneration, morality, and discipline. The humanistic versions of the fall see these things as roadblocks to man's recovery from the fall.

The essence of humanism (and the fall) is man's attempt to be his own god, determining good and evil for himself and in relationship to himself (Gen. 3:1–5). This means a denial of any objective standard of good and evil in favor of a subjective one. Good then becomes what is good *for me*, and evil is what is evil *for me*, without reference to any other standard. This means that, objectively considered, all human actions are equal or equivalent: whether a man commits murder, theft, or adultery is not itself good or evil but only insofar as it serves his needs and wishes successfully. As a result, Sartre holds

> that all human activities are equivalent (for they all tend to sacrifice man in order that the self-cause may arise) and that all are on principle doomed to failure. Thus it amounts to the same thing whether one gets drunk alone or is a leader of nations. If one of these activities takes precedence over the other, this will not be because of its real goal but because of the degree of consciousness which it possesses of its ideal goal; and in this case it will be the quietism of the solitary drunkard which will take precedence over the vain agitation of the leader of nations.[4]

---

3. See R. J. Rushdoony, *Noble Savages: Exposing the Worldview of Pornography and Their War Against Christian Civilization* (Vallecito, CA: Ross House Books, 2005).

4. Jean-Paul Sartre, *Being and Nothingness* (New York, NY: Philosophical Library,

This principle of the equality of all human action because of the absence of any trans-human norms or laws means, as Sartre points out, the *repudiation* of "the spirit of seriousness."[5] Life is no longer real nor earnest but a cosmic accident and hence to be treated as a bad joke. The spirit of seriousness is the spirit of self-consciousness, of the awareness of responsibility before God and to God. It is a knowledge of guilt in relationship to that responsibility for the fallen, or of grateful obedience for the redeemed. For those to whom the fall is from an animal oblivion to righteousness, it follows, in Seidenberg's words, "Conceivably we may return to the Garden of Eden, en masse, on pain of abandoning all knowledge of good and evil."[6]

It follows further, from this humanistic idea of man's fall, that God's law is the major roadblock to man's liberation. As a result, antinomianism is the lifeblood of the modern worldview, and this antinomianism has all but captured the churches. We have come a long way from 1663, when John Cotton, whose influence in framing the laws of Massachusetts was great, declared:

> The best form of government. To make the Lord God our Governor is the best form of government in a Christian Commonwealth...that form of government where (1) the people that have the power of choosing their governors are in covenant with God; (2) wherein the men chosen by them are godly men, and fitted with a spirit of government; (3) in which the laws they rule by are the laws of God; (4) wherein laws are executed, inheritance allotted, and civil differences are composed, according to God's appointment.[7]

Because modern humanistic education, especially since John Dewey, regards Biblical faith as the heart of man's problem, is antinomian to the core, and works to create an anthill psychology in man, it must be seen as militantly anti-Christian. The decline of Christian faith has not been accidental. A. A. Hodge was right when, almost a century ago, he predicted:

1956), p. 627.

5. ibid., p. 626.

6. Roderick Seidenberg, *Anatomy of the Future* (Chapel Hill, NC: The University of North Carolina Press, 1961), p. 58.

7. Cited in Paul S. Newman, ed., *In God We Trust* (Norwalk, CT: C. R. Gibson Company, 1974), p. 18.

I am as sure as I am of Christ's reign that a comprehensive and centralized system of national education, separated from religion, as is now commonly proposed, will prove the most appalling enginery for the propagation of anti-Christian and atheistic unbelief, and of antisocial nihilistic ethics, individual, social and political, which this sin-rent world has ever seen.[8]

As we have seen, it is not sufficient to ask whether the "fall" was up, after Darwin, or "down," after Freud. This fall was *from* original righteousness in the Lord, *from* covenant-keeping to covenant-breaking. Restoration means regeneration and obedience; it means life within the covenant. To claim adherence to the covenant and yet to give our children to the enemy to rear is Moloch worship: it is disobedience to the covenant.

Christian education, Christian schools, are thus a religious necessity. A faithful church cannot long endure or prosper without Christian schools. The church is then rootless, out of place, and simply a relic in a humanistic society. Because Biblical religion is a total faith, and our God a total and sovereign Lord, we must claim *every* area of life and thought for Christ, and the area of education is a central one, and, next to the family, most basic to the life of man. As Van Til has observed,

> Modern man has his own substitute for historic Christianity. He, not God, determines the goal of life. He must be his own standard of right and wrong. He must provide his own power of motivation.[9]

The function of the statist schools is at every point to influence the child to determine the goals of his life in independence from God, church, and family. The child is encouraged to set his own goals and to see himself as the final reference point in human experience.[10] The child is systematically separated from God and attached to humanistic society. Since Dewey, separation, alienation, or lack of attachment to any group of men is the ultimate in offense. As Van Til has noted, "The most harmful influences are those which bring ultimate separation between groups of men. Any

---

8. A. A. Hodge, *Popular Lectures on Theological Themes* (Philadelphia, PA: Presbyterian Board of Publications, 1887), pp. 283–284.

9. Cornelius Van Til, *The Dilemma of Education* (Grand Rapids, MI: National Union of Christian Schools, 1954), p. 2.

10. ibid., p. 5.

experience which is not attainable by all men is evil."[11]

The memoirs of men and women in earlier and more godly eras indicate that their youthful mental stress was over their inadequate conformity to the Word of God. Contemporary data is overwhelmingly clear that mental stress with youth and adults today is over inability to conform adequately with the words and standards of men. We miss the point if we blame motion pictures and television for this problem: it existed before they arrived on the scene, although they have aggravated the problem. The real cause is an anti-Christian system of education which, because it is humanistic in essence, predisposes modern man to be conformed to man rather than to God. We cannot be systematically and truly conformed to God as a people until our education is conformed to Him also. This means Christian schools.

---

11. ibid., p. 7.

Chapter 2

THE COVENANT: WITH GOD OR MAN?

SATAN HAS BEEN described as the ape of God, meaning that all that the creature can do is predetermined by God, and all possibility and potentiality is of God's ordination. When the rebellious creature seeks independence from God, his every act is an imitation of the God he rejects, and all his possibilities are of God's creation.

In creating man, God established the covenant of grace whereby the conditions of man's life, and the laws of his personal and social existence, were ordained by God and set forth in His inscriptured Word. The covenant thus establishes the laws of man's being, his relationship to God and to man, and departure from the covenant means that the processes of death begin to work in man and society.

Because all the possibilities of life are God-created, man cannot in his rebellion do more than try to appropriate the conditions of God's creation without God Himself. As a result, man, although a covenant-breaker with God, finds that he cannot live without a covenant, and he attempts to replace God's covenant with a man-made one. The Enlightenment replaced the idea of the covenant with the doctrine of the social contract, a humanistic parody of Reformed doctrine. However, in pagan antiquity, without the term "social contract," men rationalized their attempts at social order as some kind of covenant or contract with their gods. These polytheistic social contracts were in essence humanistic, in that the focus in all was on man, and the standard was at all times man. True, the definition of man was usually very limited, being restricted to a race, nation, or even an office or ruler, but it was still man who was at the center. The social contract or covenant was by man and essentially with man. The Greek gods, we should remember, were deified men. The idea of some form of social contract has been implicit in all cultures, simply because *society means community, and there can be no community without communion.* It is not an accident that the basic rite or sacrament of the covenant is called *communion.* It is communion with the Lord of the covenant by His grace, and communion between man and men who are in that grace.

Society without communion falls apart. The builders of Babel, smitten by God, lost elementary communion in the form of a common language, and they were scattered by their loss of communion.

In earlier eras, and still in many cultures, communion rested on blood ties, i.e., being of one family, clan, or tribe. In a broader sense, this still applies, although the definition of family has been expanded. All Frenchmen are ostensibly of one family, although they include Bretons, Franks, Basques, and many others, and the common language for some is an imposed foreign language. The internationalists speak of all men as being of one blood and *therefore* of necessity one community, which is simply an expansion of the earlier tribal and racial definition of community. Socially and intellectually, these arguments fail. Community and communion are not natural products of blood. The first murder, after all, was between brothers.

Man needs community to live in peace, but his every attempt to form a covenant which will provide communion is a failure. The problems of the national and international covenants are all around us. A major modern attempt to ensure a covenant of peace between man and man is education, humanistic, statist education. The goal of education, according to most of the twentieth-century philosophers of education, is to provide the democratic experience whereby man can live in community with man.

One of the main objections against Christian schools is that they are divisive and antidemocratic. John Dewey, in *A Common Faith*, saw Christianity as divisive because of its religious and moral discrimination between the saved and the lost, between good and evil. The purpose of such humanistic education is thus communion without God, communion beyond good and evil. Only as the distinctions are abandoned between regenerate and unregenerate, between good and evil, between races and sexes, between any and all facts of creation which might posit a difference or a barrier, can community be realized, we are told.

The humanistic covenant of life, therefore, requires the abandonment of Biblical faith as having the savor of death and divisiveness. Communion is held to rest on a radical independence from truth, because there is no truth in a world of brute factuality, a world without God. Christians are ridiculed for separating themselves from the world of evil, and for establishing small and separated churches in terms of the whole counsel of God, because truth is held to be meaningless, subjective, or irrelevant, whereas man's unity is held to be paramount.

However, the closer humanistic education comes to its ideal of an amoral, nontheistic family-of-man covenant, the more nearly it approaches total anarchy rather than community. In April 1975, a U.S. Senate subcommittee stated that vandalism in state schools now costs about half a billion dollars a year and the lives of a hundred murdered students; there is also extensive rape, robbery, and assault on school premises. Is this communion? The humanistic covenant of life is rather a covenant of death.

It is not an accident that Christian schools are also called covenant schools, because the function they discharge is a covenant task. Covenant schools require *communion in the truth*. For them, there is no compromise between good and evil, truth and error. Jesus Christ, the Truth, requires a separation unto Himself in the totality of our being, so that our lives, callings, thinking, and acting are to be governed by His Word. Every area of life and thought must be brought into submissions to Christ and His Word.

The principle of the fall is that every man is his own god, knowing or determining good and evil for himself (Gen. 3:5). Every man as his own god means anarchy, and the efforts of humanism are designed to protect and bolster man's anarchic independence from God while finding some ground for the communion of man with man. But where man declares his independence from God, he will not hesitate to declare his independence from man also, and the result is radical anarchy. Moreover, God being denied, objective and ultimate truth is also denied, and education then affirms merely the principle of change. Because man is ultimate, all else is relative and changing. Every man becomes his own universe, and is at war with all other men. As a result, humanistic education is contemptuous of subject matter. It talks of teaching the child, not the subject. It despises factuality, because its world has only one fact, autonomous, anarchic man.

Covenant man, however, lives as God's creature in a universe totally created by God. The world therefore has total meaning. There are not brute or meaningless facts in the universe, only God-created facts. As a result, every subject is theologically governed and religiously interpreted. Only the faithful covenant man can be a consistent and true teacher, because he alone does justice to the facts. Because he is in the covenant of grace, he is in communion with God and therefore open to the universe of meaning. Because he is in communion with God, he is also in communion with other covenant men and has the principles of peace and truth as his guide and mainstay.

The function of the humanistic "public" schools has been to establish the covenant of the "family of man." To commit our children to such schools is to surrender them to an anti-Christian covenant, in violation of our baptismal vows. Communion and community are not in man nor of man, but of God through Christ. The covenant of grace requires covenant schools, because only God makes both communion and education possible. To deny the sovereign and triune God is to deny the possibility of either community or learning, because it leaves only an anarchistic man in a meaningless universe. Because this anarchistic man wants a world beyond good and evil, and beyond any meaning other than his own autonomy and ultimacy, he will reduce all men and all things to meaninglessness. Having declared himself to be god, autonomous man will allow no other gods before him and will be at total war with God, man, and meaning. To say this is to describe the course of modern history.

Chapter 3

EDUCATION & THE DEATH OF MAN

ABOUT SIX YEARS ago, a young woman, taking university courses in education, told me of a lecture by the dean of the school. The dean stressed the need to separate education from the bondage to subject matter. Every area of study, he insisted, is subject to such rapid change that to teach a child in terms of the knowledge of today is to handicap the future of that mind by harnessing it to what will soon be obsolete learning or information. The need, he said, is to educate for change, for perpetual change or revolution, since no point of fixity exists, and change is the only permanent and constant factor in the universe.

A logical question then follows: if education is into the fact of change, what content is there, then, in education? Do we not then have a contentless education, devoid of meaning and data? In a sense, we do, as we face the world. All things are reduced to change and have no other content. All factuality as change or flux is equally meaningful and equally meaningless. However, a constant factor still remains, the ostensibly autonomous mind of man, which, as final judge and arbiter, pronounces all things to be change and thereby defines them. By reducing all things else to meaninglessness, man establishes his mind as ultimate in an isolation of chaos.

An example of this was a discussion among scientists who were responsible for the space flight to the moon about the theoretical impossibility of their work. Although their mathematical calculations had pinpointed a man on the moon, they were theoretically incredulous at this fact. How the logic of man's mind, as expressed mathematically, could have any correlation to the world of nature, which is a world of brute factuality and change, was to them a mystery. For the Christian, there is no problem. God as the Creator of all things, is the creator therefore of the material world as well as of man's mind. There is a correlation between man's mathematical logic and the physical universe because they alike possess a common Creator whose laws undergird and bind together all of reality. However, lacking such a faith, Dr. Remo J. Ruffini, a physicist at Princeton, could declare:

> How a mathematical structure can correspond to nature is a mystery. One way out is just to say that the language in which nature speaks is the language of mathematics. This begs the question. Often we are both shocked and surprised by the correspondence between mathematics and nature, especially when the experiment confirms that our mathematical model describes nature perfectly.[1]

Dr. Ruffini confesses himself to be "shocked" by the correlation, which he subsequently admits could be solved by positing God, but it does not make him repentant. Apparently, it is preferable to deny the theoretical possibility of a correlation and meaning than to admit the reality of the Creator God.

The essence of the anti-Biblical position with respect to knowledge is that it is necessary to understand in order to believe. This position is basic to Greek philosophy, Scholasticism, modern philosophy, and all other forms of humanism. The end result of this insistence on autonomous understanding is no understanding at all, and men like Ruffini, who are a part of one of the most spectacular of scientific feats, deny that what they have done can be understood.

The Biblical position with respect to knowledge was succinctly set forth by St. Anselm: "I do not seek to understand that I may believe, but I believe in order to understand. For this also I believe, — that unless I believed, I should not understand."[2]

The starting point of Christian education is therefore faith and covenant obedience, whereas the starting and ending point of humanistic education is doubt. The starting point of faith means that we accept the universe as God's creation and therefore know that valid knowledge of

---

1. "The Princeton Galaxy," interviews by Florence Helitzer, *Intellectual Digest*, June 1973, no. 10: p. 3.

2. St. Anselm, "Proslogium," in Deane, pp. 6–7.

that universe is possible. Because of the fact of creation, there is a total consistency between all parts, and there is a correlation between the logic of mathematics and the facts of nature. Every subject thus is only consistently understandable on Biblical premises.

Remember Sartre's denial of "the spirit of seriousness," and his insistence that the truest existentialist or humanist is the drunkard who is totally oblivious of everything except himself. The *logic* of humanism requires us to learn nothing because no fact has any objective validity, and we are most faithful to humanism when we "do our own thing" in total disregard for God, man, and nature. The counsel of Greek philosophy, "Know thyself," finally becomes the *only* possible knowledge for humanistic man. The problem, then, is that man cannot know himself in a world without meaning, because there is no criterion for knowledge, discernment, or judgment. In fact, man finds it impossible to be totally humanistic this side of hell. As Erica Jong, an existentialist, admits with deadly accuracy, "The trouble with existentialism is that you can't stop thinking about the future. Actions *do* have consequences."[3] To admit consequences is to deny man's autonomy and ultimacy.

Humanistic education, by denying meaning to the world around us, not only denies knowledge but also denies man, because man cannot live in a vacuum. He is a creature: he is not self-sufficient, and, for man to deny God is to deny himself also. It has, after all, been not only Van Til but humanists also who have pointed out that the logical conclusion of the Death of God idea is the death of man. A. Malraux has seen the connection;[4] Michel Foucault has also proclaimed the coming death of man.[5] We are at the end of an era, the age of humanism, and humanistic man is proclaiming his own imminent death.

It is urgent, therefore, for Christians to proclaim the rebirth of man in Christ and the rebirth of society through Christian education. In a world of dying men, the living will command the day. It is imperative, therefore,

---

3. Erica Jong, *Fear of Flying*, p. 250.

4. E. W. Knight, *Literature Considered as Philosophy* (New York, NY: Collier Books, 1962), p. 182.

5. Roy McMullen, "Michel Foucault," in *Horizon*, 11, no. 4, (Autumn 1969): p. 37. See also R. J. Rushdoony, *The Word of Flux* (Fairfax, VA: Thoburn Press, 1975).

that mature Christians be reared to exercise dominion in every area of life and thought. Most Christians today are immature and unlearned in terms of covenant knowledge, and as a result are ineffectual Christians. It is interesting that one of the New Testament Greek words translated as "unlearned" or "ignorant" is literally in the Greek *idiotes*. Its modern meaning is a departure from its original meaning, but there is a valid connection. Unlearned or "idiot" Christianity is ignorant of the faith, and ignorant of the necessary connection between every area of life and thought and the presuppositions of Biblical faith. Without the sovereign and triune God, no knowledge is possible except on the borrowed premises of Biblical faith. With faith in the God of Scripture, a thorough Christian education, and the development of its meaning for every area of life, is *mandatory*. Christians have an obligation to develop grade schools, high schools, colleges, universities, and graduate schools. The idea of the *university* is a Christian one, and it cannot long exist without a faith in one God, one universe created by Him, and a totally unified and interrelated law structure in that universe. Without that faith, the *unity, certainty,* and *consistency* of knowledge disappear.

Just as humanistic education is leading to the death of humanistic man, so a truly Christian education alone offers life to man and society in and through Christ.

Chapter 4

CONFLICT & RESISTANCE

IT IS IMPORTANT for us to look briefly at the legal situation with respect to Christianity and Christian schools. Since I am not a lawyer, my perspective will be historical and theological.

We must remember, as we approach the framing of the U.S. Constitution of 1787, that, at that time, the idea of a secular or humanistic state was relatively unknown. It was the French Revolution which first disestablished Christianity in the Western world. The normal question was not, "Shall the state be Christian?" but, rather, "Which church shall be the established church of the state?" A major factor in the American War of Independence was the American rejection of this second question. According to Bridenbaugh, "It is indeed high time that we repossess the important historical truth that religion was a fundamental cause of the American Revolution."[1] The great fear of the colonies, each of which had their own religious establishment, was that Episcopal bishops would be sent to the colonies to force the English establishment on the Americans.

This fear of a central establishment remained after the war, and the Constitution thus was silent on the subject of religion. The central government was simply a *federal* union of states which retained their own powers to decide on all key issues. Even the avoidance of the subject of religion was not enough for the clergy of the new country. Except for the Episcopalian and some Congregationalist clergymen, most favored no establishment. Certainly, *federal* establishment was not wanted: the decision belonged to the states. As a result, the First Amendment was framed to quieten the fears of the clergy. Having recently avoided the danger of an

---

1. Carl Bridenbaugh, *Mitre and Sceptre: Transatlantic Faiths, Ideas, Personalities, and Politics, 1689–1775* (New York, NY: Oxford University Press, 1962), p. xiv.

establishment imposed from Britain, the clergy and the laity had no desire to have one closer at hand in the federal power. Article or Amendment X barred the federal government from all powers not delegated to it by the Constitution. Amendment I stated:

> Congress shall make no law respecting an establishment of religion, or prohibiting the free exercise thereof; or abridging the freedom of speech, or of the press; or the right of the people peaceably to assemble, and to petition the government for a redress of grievances.

The purpose of this amendment was to retain for the states their power to establish a church. In fact, all the original states had either an established church or recognized Christianity as the established religion. Established churches steadily gave way to the establishment of Christianity per se.

Every political order, we should remember, is an establishment of religion because every political order is a *law order*. All law is an expression of moral concern or establishes procedures for the enforcement of that moral concern. Morality, moreover, is the relational and social aspect of a religious faith, establishing the faith's requirements for all communication and community between God and man, if a supernatural God is affirmed, and between man and man. Ethics is an aspect of theology. Law is thus inseparable from theology. Law is the expressed will of the god of a faith, whether that god be man or a transcendental being. Every state or law order is thus an establishment of religion.

In the United States, humanism has steadily whittled away at the Christian establishment. It has professed a belief in a neutral establishment, which is an impossibility. A state without an established religion is a state without law, an impossibility. Those civil governments professing no establishment of religion are in fact practicing a deception while they progressively establish humanism.

When the essential civil government of the United States was transferred from the states to the federal government, the federal government made clear its Christian establishment; the chaplaincy became stronger, Indian children were required to learn about Christian faith to be Americanized, the U.S. Supreme Court called the U.S. a Christian country, and so on.

In recent years, however, the United States has seen a progressive establishment of humanism. Justice Blackmun in the abortion ruling of the U.S. Supreme Court, cited pagan and humanistic religious authorities and avoided the truly Christian. Neither the courts nor the schools have been neutral: they have been radically and systematically humanistic.

In recent years, the Fourteenth Amendment has been used to interfere with a state's jurisdiction over its own religious character. The prohibition of the First Amendment has been transferred from Congress to the states, while the federal government has steadily, with the coordinate action of many states, worked to establish humanism. The meaning of the First Amendment has thus been turned upside down.

The Christian today, as in the days of Rome, is dealing with a state which denies that there is any conflict even while it persecutes the Christian, a state which says that the Christian's life and existence must be on its terms, and which affirms another god while denying that it is hostile to Christianity. How shall the Christian act in relation to the state?

It is almost impossible to counsel any kind of resistance without being told that it is in violation of Romans 13:1–10. In fact, I was once told in writing that my criticisms of the Federal Reserve System violated Romans 13! We must remember, however, that neither Paul nor his successors stopped preaching their "illegal" gospel. They obeyed the state in matters of taxation (tribute and custom), honor (respect for officers of the state), compliance to laws and standards, and so on, but they refused to abandon the propagation of the faith in any way. Rome was ready to recognize Christianity as a legal, taxable religion under Caesar's authority, but Christians denied the right of Caesar to tax or control Christ's domain, nor was Christ's Kingdom for them subject to recognition by Caesar. Caesar was dependent on and the creature of Christ, not vice versa.

Briefly, the Christians believed that, because "there is no power but of God" (Rom. 13:1), our basic and primary obedience is to God, not the state, to Christ, not Caesar. Paul, in asking that we obey civil rulers, does not ask us to be their creatures. They are ministers of God, God's ministry of justice, but they are not God.

In terms of this, it is a sin for the Christian school to seek state approval of its existence as a school. The civil authority, where it regulates a building as a building per se, i.e., for sanitary facilities, fire protection, and the like, is to be obeyed, whether or not the law is to us a sound one. It is general legislation applicable to all public buildings. However, where the state seeks to license, accredit, control, or in any way govern the Christian school as a school, it is then another question. It is a usurpation of power by the state, *and* it involves the control of one religion, Christianity, by another, humanism.

Because education is a religious activity, it is not the proper province of a state which claims to be democratic. It is then the imposition of the religion of one religious group upon another. The school, moreover, is a separate sphere under God from church and state, and it thrives most when free from both. It then serves, not an institution, but its faith.

The argument is often heard that, without "public" schools, millions could not afford to educate their children. The fact is, however, that, just as voluntary gifts provide churches sufficient to house all Americans, so too schools can be provided for all the same way. In fact, in the early years of this republic, Christians provided remarkably good help to immigrants and schools for their children at a time when immigrants were pouring into the country. The major cost of all education, from kindergarten through graduate school, is still provided by families, not the civil government.

The term "secular humanism" is deceptive to many and leads them to conclude that such humanism is nonreligious. The dictionary definition of *secular* throws light on its meaning. *Secular* has four basic meanings: two do not apply (1. brought about in the course of ages; 2. occurring or observed only once in an age or century). Two do apply: 1. pertaining to this present world and life, contrasted with *religious* or *spiritual*; 2. one in holy orders who is not bound by monastic vows. Secular humanism is that form of the humanistic faith which is not ecclesiastical but is out in the world, applying its faith to the problems of this life in terms of humanistic standards. The "worldliness" of secular humanism makes it no less a religious faith.

In this faith, man is not the creature of the triune God, made in His image, but the product of a natural world who evolved out of a primordial accident of life. Instead of being God's ordained dominion man over creation (Gen. 1:26–28), man is the subject of that creation. According to Dr. Oleg Szczepski, a Marxist pediatrician in Poland, "The environment is decisive." "In other words young people are what we have brought them up to be."[2] In such a view, it becomes the duty of the scientific socialist state and its schools to provide that decisive environment and remake man into the desired image. This same sense of duty is present in the educators of the democratic humanist state. It involves a strong sense of mission and dedication, but an ungodly one. Christians today must manifest a like sense of mission and dedication for the Lord. John Dewey held that the school has the power and duty to modify the social order. It is the principle agent for the creation and development of the "Great Community."

It is the humanists today who have the compelling sense of mission. Christians must regain their world-conquering mission or perish. The Christian school is basic to that calling. The humanists have understood that the school is the key: it is time for the Christians to recognize this also.

---

2. Oleg Szczepski, "The Environment Is Decisive," *Poland*, no. 7 (263) (July 1976): p. 25.

Chapter 5

THE SOVEREIGNTY OF
GOD IN EDUCATION

ALTHOUGH OUR EVIDENCE is at times fragmentary, one of the more interesting areas of study in the early church is with respect to church membership. Both the latitude and the severity of standards are surprising to us at first glance. The first epistle of St. Paul to the Corinthians shows us that some new members still held to the Greek belief that sins of the flesh were meaningless, because only the spirit is religiously significant; they boasted of their "freedom" in matters of the flesh (1 Cor. 5:1–2). On the other hand, the swift reaction of St. Paul was to require and secure the excommunication of the offender (1 Cor. 5:13) and then his restoration on repentance (2 Cor. 2:6–11).

In the Council of Ancyra, A.D. 314, we see how seriously sin was regarded, and members in sin were barred from full communion for a long period of time as a penalty for their offenses: seven years for adultery, ten years for abortion, and so on; repentant murderers were granted full communion only on their deathbed. Capital offenses which the state did not punish with death the church thus punished with a long reminder of the seriousness of their offense. The practice of divination, magic, sorcery, or the like, meant a five-year suspension.

One of the arguments which divided the early church had reference to the return after persecutions of members who denied Christ when faced with death. The church as a whole favored restoration upon due process, while dividing groups rejected their return.

Another problem which troubled the church was *the vocation* of members. Could a soldier, a judge, an imperial official, or various other peoples be Christians? The modern attitude is to dismiss this question by

108

referring to Philippians 4:22, "All the saints salute you, chiefly they that are of Caesar's household." The reference is probably to men who were of high-ranking positions in the management of Caesar's realms. They were Christians in good standing, and ostensibly this should settle the question. Not quite. We do know that, while all legitimate vocations were godly callings, many men in such vocations, when required to do that which went against their conscience, resigned, witnessed against the orders, and died for their faith. The justified man had to justify his calling in terms of God's Word and its usefulness to the Kingdom of God. There was a strong sense of kingdom responsibility which we must not ignore. We must not idealize the early church: it had serious problems and errors, was often infected with Greek philosophies, had problems with weak and ignorant converts, and was often faced with internal tensions. What did emphatically mark it as strong in a dying and atomistic world was its very strong sense of being a new humanity in Christ, the new and victorious race born of the last Adam, and therefore a community with strong ties one to another. Williams, while calling attention to the aberrations of the early church, still affirms it to have been a remarkable church:

> Had the Day of Judgment come to pass in those days, the majority of believers would have been placed on the King's right hand. The sick and the poor were cared for, and work was found for the unemployed. Strangers were entertained as brothers in Christ. Those who had lost all rather than to deny their faith, were given shelter and support. Our annual sunrise service was a daily concern, for every day brought its Easter message. One's private life belonged to a community of saints and was fashioned by its decrees and sustained by its resources. The home was also claimed as a spiritual reservoir to nurture the family in the love and fear of the Lord. They were citizens of the Kingdom of God and the greatest benefactors of the State.[1]

The sense of community was intensely strong. The anti-Christian emperor, Julian, declared, "These godless Galileans feed not only their own poor but ours; our poor lack care."

The early church took seriously the words of St. Paul in 1 Corinthians

---

1. Robert R. Williams, *A Guide to the Teachings of the Early Church Fathers* (Grand Rapids, MI: William B. Eerdmans, 1960), p. 131.

7:20–23. *First*, godly men are not revolutionists: the Lord's way is regeneration, not revolution. Hence, a frontal assault, for example, on slavery was forbidden. *Second*, if possible, they should seek freedom honestly as the best condition for God's freemen. *Third*, as Christ's servants or slaves, bought with a price, they could not voluntarily enslave themselves to men.

As a result, while Christians could be office-bearers under Caesar, they were servants of Christ alone. They could not, unlike modern office-bearers, see themselves as servants of the people, or servants of the state. They were *Christ's servants*, "bought with a price."

The early church had serious weaknesses which far surpass those of the church today, but its strength was far greater. There was a reason for this. *First*, as Williams has pointed out, the faithful were a community, and a responsible community. *Second*, the early church was aware of its *conflict with the world*; now, there is little sense of conflict. It would not occur to a church, its officers, or its members today to raise such questions as these: Is a judge who does not challenge the humanistic law which is taking over our country faithful to Christ? Is he the servant of the people, or the state, or is he Christ's servant? Is a union member who does not work against the humanistic and coercive tactics of the unions faithful to the Lord? Can employers and workers disregard Ephesians 6:5–9 and be counted as godly? We do not yet accept pimps and prostitutes into church membership, but can we legitimately accept antinomians who assume that a verbal profession of faith can replace a disavowal of Christ in their works?

Above all, can we retain in membership people who affirm Christ as Lord and Savior and yet turn over their children to a godless school? There was a time when most churches said no; a few still go through the formality of asking members to remember their obligation to bring up their children in the Lord, but it is no longer a ground for excommunication. And yet the Scripture repeatedly requires us to teach the law-word of God to our children (Deut. 6:7, 20–25). The Scripture requires, in fact, the death penalty for Moloch worship (Lev. 18:21; 20:2). St. Stephen cited this fact of Moloch worship as one of the great evils of Israel (Acts 7:43).

It is important for us to understand the meaning of Moloch (or, Molech) worship. The actual word is *Melek, king*, but the Hebrew prophets deliberately misvocalized it, introducing the vowels of the Hebrew word for *shame*. Melek, Moloch, or Milcom, or literally, the king, was the god of the Ammonites and other peoples. This religion affirmed, not the sovereignty of the God of Scripture, but the godhood of the state and its ruler. Passing children through the fire to Moloch was human sacrifice, and it is this dramatic aspect of the faith which most people remember, without thinking about its meaning. Only on rare occasions were such human sacrifices of children required. In principle, they affirmed the absolute lordship of the king who had the right to take *anything* when his need required it. *The human sacrifice set forth his title to all the children at all times.* They belonged to the state, to be taught the faith of the state, to die for the state, to work for the state, and, in all things, to be the creatures of their king, Moloch. Thus, the heart of Moloch worship was not the human sacrifice by blood but the human sacrifice in daily submission to the king as absolute lord and sovereign.

The Biblical answer to Moloch for the man of faith comes early. God as absolute sovereign affirmed His right to demand the life of Isaac from Abraham (Gen. 22). Abraham agreed to this, and he was blessed of God. God did not require the death of Isaac, but He did make clear thereby His absolute right to the life of every child of the covenant. Our children belong to God, not to man, neither to the father (such as Abraham), nor to the Moloch state.

The issue today is Moloch worship. The very reason for the establishment of state schools has been, since the days of Horace Mann, the control of man by the state.[2] As early as 1788, Jonathan Jackson, an advocate in New England of statist education, wrote, in his *Thoughts Upon the Political Situation of the United States*, against the idea of private schools and privately owned newspapers; state ownership was his gospel. He held that society must be one large family with the elite ruler as its father.[3] This, of course, is simply the thesis of the Moloch society. The kingship of Christ is replaced by the kingship of man.

This evil is compounded by the fact that supposed Christians are today

---

2. See Rushdoony, *The Messianic Character of American Education* (Nutley, NJ: The Craig Press, [1963] 1972).

3. See Murray Rothbard, "Historical Origins," in William F. Rickenbacker, ed., *The Twelve-Year Sentence* (La Salle, IL: Open Court, 1974), p. 15.

separating lordship from salvation and denying Christ's lordship before the millennium. Such a view is a denial of Christ, who is emphatically declared by Scripture to be "the Lord Jesus" (Rom. 10:9, etc.). Moreover, St. Paul in 1 Corinthians 12:3 declares,

> Wherefore I give you to understand, that no man speaking by the Spirit of God calleth Jesus accursed: and that no man can say that Jesus is the Lord, but by the Holy Ghost.

This makes it clear that, if men deny that "Jesus is the Lord," they do *not* speak "by the Spirit of God" but by another spirit.

The roots of our problem today are in part in the Manichaean influence on the church. Manichaeanism divided reality into two realms, the spiritual under the good god, and the material under the bad god. Whatever one did in the material realm was by nature alien and irrelevant to righteousness. This reduced marriage, incest, and homosexuality to the same level in theory and at times in practice. It meant also that the lordship of the good god was limited to the spiritual realm, and involvement by his people in the material realm was to be avoided and meant a compromise with evil.

Under the influence of Neoplatonic and Manichaean ideas, the church has in recent years withdrawn from the world, withdrawn from education, politics, science, the arts, and all things else. It has thereby denied the lordship of Christ Jesus.

In Jeremiah 31:31–34, we have a prophecy of the new covenant in Christ and its end results. In verse 34, we are told,

> And they shall teach no more every man his neighbour, and every man his brother, saying, Know the LORD: for they shall all know me, from the least of them unto the greatest of them, saith the LORD: for I will forgive their iniquity, and I will remember their sin no more.

This is a vision of a world in which basic evangelism is no longer necessary, because all men have a knowledge of the Lord. Such a world order is not possible without Christian schools, schools which teach every subject in terms of Biblical presuppositions and which give also a systematic study of the whole Word of God to every child.

The sovereignty of God in education requires us to reorganize all education in terms of Biblical faith and presuppositions, to assert the crown rights of King Jesus in every area of life and thought, and to yield unto our Lord His due obedience in church, state, school, home, vocation, and in all of life. Nothing short of this is Christian. The doctrine of God's sovereignty requires it.

Chapter 6

CHRISTIAN EDUCATION &
THE UNIVERSITY

CULTURE IS RELIGION externalized, and every culture represents a faith in action. To understand a culture, it is necessary to understand its basic religious premises and motives.

In understanding the religious foundations of a culture, very often its formal religious institutions are the least rewarding source of insight. Temple, church, synagogue, and shrine can function as cultural relics sometimes long after their relevance is gone. Thus, in some European countries, as many as 99 percent of all the people are baptized, a high percentage are confirmed, and a very low percentage believe and practice the Christian faith.

Two areas of any civilization will give us ready index to the faith of the people. These two areas are *law* and *education*. All law is either an implicitly enacted morality and represents moral norms in its procedures, counts, and officers, or it is an open and explicit enactment of a religious code of morality. Whether implicitly or explicitly, it is a moral code, and that moral code rests on a religious premise, on a doctrine of ultimacy or theodicy. Every legal structure is thus inescapably an establishment of religion, and, historically, the most important and most dominant form of religious establishment. The religious foundations of Western law have been Christian. They are in process of being disestablished, and humanism is in process of becoming the established religion of most states in the world today. Christianity, Shintoism, Buddhism, Mohammedanism, Hinduism, and other faiths are being steadily disestablished, their laws discarded, and humanistic laws established instead.

The same is true of education. The power to educate is being taken from church and family and controlled and administered by the state. The established religion of the state schools, as witness Dewey's *A Common Faith*, is the religion of humanity, humanism. In this area, the new religion is facing a strong challenge in the growth of the Christian school movement.

It is significant that the challenge to the new faith comes in education. The modern idea of *the school*, in particular as it comes in focus in the *university*, is very plainly Christian. The classical world had a few academies, but the idea of the university was alien to it. The presupposition of the university is a universe, a unified entity. This is clearly the world created by one God, with one law, and one universe. From top to bottom, there is a unity. Truth is the same everywhere, because God created all things. Mars and Venus do not have another system of truth than we do. This seems so obvious to us, that we forget that this concept is alien to antiquity, and increasingly alien to many in our midst. Clark Kerr, as president of the University of California, denied the idea of a universe in favor of a multiverse. He denied a unifying truth in favor of the equal validity or invalidity of all ideas. One practical consequence was the granting of a degree in witchcraft.

The classical world was largely polytheistic; it believed in a multiverse. There were many gods and many truths. No truth belonged in common to all creation, nor any god. One consequence of this position was a two-headed opinion which still affects us. *First*, in a polytheistic world, there is no sovereign God over all things, and no absolute good and evil. A man may choose or create his own gods and his moral options. Intellectually, this provided the roots for the doctrine of academic freedom. No opinion or teaching has any more claim to validity or truth than any other. All opinions and ideas are equally valid and equally false. Ideas or universals do not exist in matter or the material world as such. They are the perception by man of abstract concepts. Progress requires the imposition of the idea or form upon matter. The Greek city-states, often widely different in nature, and Rome, were thus ideas in action.

Second, while this idea meant the implicit equality of all ideas, and hence academic freedom, it also meant imperialism. In a multiverse, in a polytheistic realm or cosmos, no idea has any inherent necessity. No idea is basic to the nature of things. Its extension, thus, is by imposition and by imperialism. Polytheism thus, in both ancient and modern forms, is imperialistic. Our age thus holds to an anarchistic doctrine of academic freedom and works harder than all others to impose ideas on others. This should not surprise us. Anarchism requires imperialism: there is no possible communication through a given common realm of truth.

A Christian in an academic setting faces therefore a peculiar assault. Because he believes in a binding truth on all men, he is an enemy of academic freedom. At the same time, because he is not open to the equality of good and evil, truth and error, he will not compromise. He is thus the target of academic and administrative imperialism. Since he will not be reduced to the common level of pragmatism and expediency, he is the target of bulldozing activities.

To resist this assault, he must gain epistemological self-consciousness; he must be aware of his theological roots. Christian education presupposes one God, one law, one truth, one universe. The Christian educator does not claim to *have* the absolute truth, but he insists that truth is absolute, and it is real. His body of truth has its canon, the Scriptures, as the rule of faith and practice. To teach a discipline from a Christian perspective therefore means to presuppose, not a polytheistic multiverse, but the triune God as Lord and Creator. It means that the world is not a product of man's will and idea but of God's creative fiat. It means that there is a universe of coherency and meaning, that, instead of brute or unintelligible and meaningless factuality, we have a universe of total meaning, because it is totally the handiwork of God. The universe is not only a universe of meaning but of law. There is *necessity* in that law and meaning, violations of which produce unhappy consequences. That order of necessity comes from God, not man.

Where we place *necessity* will determine our society, our education, and our culture. If we place necessity in man, we will have totalitarian man and his tyrant state. If we place necessity in God, we deny it to man, and culture and its education will stress the law structure of reality rather than the law structure of the state. We will teach history, predestination by God, not social science, predestination by man. We will teach economics, the fact of necessity in the nature of things, rather than political economics, with necessity transferred to the state.

In brief, we will have radically opposed premises and conclusions.

Part IV

Chapter 1

THE PHILOSOPHY OF DISCIPLINE

BEFORE WE CAN discuss the meaning of *discipline*, it is very necessary to make it clear that it must not be confused with *chastisement*. Both words need careful definition. *Chastise* comes from the Latin *castus*, pure, chaste, and is related to *chastity*. *Chastisement* is not the same as *punishment*, which is a matter of *retribution*. Chastisement is corrective and merciful in purpose. Its meaning is very clear in Hebrews 12:5–11. Chastening is there set forth as evidence of the Father's love and concern for His sons and His correction of them.

The word *discipline* is close to the word *disciple*. It means to make a disciple of someone, to drill and educate him or her, and to bring him or her into effective obedience to someone or something.

Chastisement without discipline is ineffective. Too many parents think that, by beating their children or scolding them endlessly, they will thereby discipline them effectively. Unless someone is first of all disciplined, chastisement accomplishes nothing. All that remains for that person is punishment and judgment.

Discipline is instruction and guidance into an orderly way of life which becomes second nature to the person involved. Army discipline used to be definable in those terms. In terms of the older and now obsolete army discipline, a soldier was trained and drilled to the point where his responses to certain situations, orders, and crises would be automatic. It used to be commonplace for well-trained soldiers to describe how, in a critical situation, they reacted instantly and did all the right things without having a chance to think about them. Good, disciplined car drivers do the same: in a crisis, they react instantly and correctly before they realize that they have done so.

Christian discipline is similar. The child is systematically trained in

119

the faith, in knowledge of the Bible and its requirements, in every necessary area of study, and so thoroughly imbued with all of this that it is a part of his nature. He acts and reacts in terms of this.

Christian discipline is a necessary part of sanctification. Basic to it is regeneration. It is the regenerate man who is best disciplined, because he has the foundation, a new nature, which is in full harmony with the discipline required of him. The more he grows in terms of that discipline, the more useful he becomes to His Lord.

However, even without regeneration, Christian discipline accomplishes much. We know that in 1815 the average age of criminals in the United States was forty-five; it took a person some years, however unregenerate, to throw off the discipline of the then universal Christian schooling. On the other hand, adults who today are converted but have a background of undisciplined home and school life usually have an insuperable handicap to overcome. A man who can barely read and write, and whose ability to organize and order his life is almost nil, becomes, when converted, a redeemed child of God, but a very ineffective one.

Christian discipline requires the cooperation of the church, home, and school. The church is a seriously weak point in this situation. Sunday school discipline is usually weak, and chastisement is lacking. The adult church members are themselves undisciplined, and the church teaches little to remedy the situation. *Godly sanctification requires discipline.* Too many pastors and churches prefer to substitute enthusiasm for discipline, and this aggravates the problem, because nothing can take the place of discipline. In enthusiasm, I am sovereign, not God; I become excited about something, and I respond to it: it is my choice. In Christian discipline, I know that, because I belong to the Lord, it is my duty, privilege, and joy to do that which God requires of me. I act as a disciple, not as a lord.

It is the duty of the church to teach discipline and discipleship. Parents and children need to be instructed in the meaning and requirements of discipline systematically. In almost all churches today, a high percentage of the children and youth show an obvious lack of discipline.

The Christian school should encourage friendly churches to teach and preach on discipline. There are many excellent texts in Scripture on the subject, especially in Deuteronomy and Proverbs. Consider Proverbs 22:6,

"Train up a child in the way he should go: and when he is old, he will not depart from it." Lists of verses, information on the Christian school, and a note on the need for church, home, and school to work together to teach discipline should go to churches annually.

Parents need to be told that they are not paying the Christian school to take over the problems of education and discipline from their hands but to assist the parent in that task. Written statements, not only of policy, but of cooperation, should go to all parents. Parents emphatically do not like to be told how to handle their own children, so any statement requires tact and intelligence. It should be stressed that discipline requires the cooperation of church, school, and family. Each has its own distinctive task and cannot infringe on the other.

The school, to discharge its own responsibility with respect to discipline, must itself be disciplined. This too is often lacking. The better schools seek continually to grow in their ability to teach, in their knowledge of subjects, and in their own faith. Some schools hold annual teachers' meetings to work on the improvement of instruction; others take part in regional conferences. In one way or another, the school has an obligation to be disciplined. Undisciplined schools and teachers cannot be productive of disciplined students.

Moreover, discipline is not into the life of the family, the church, or the school, but into life under God, wherever we are. We are told, of Hebrew education in the light of Scripture, that its purpose is "to educate the child in order to fit him to be a servant of God; it is education of children for God."[1] Early Roman education, on the other hand, "was not the transmission of knowledge; it was the transmission of tradition."[2] Our discipline is a failure if its essential nature is a transmission of a tradition, Presbyterian, Baptist, Episcopal, or whatever you choose. The tradition may be a good one, but the purpose of discipline should be a greater goal, discipleship in Christ. Towards this discipline, church, school, and home each have their distinctive contribution to make, to prepare the child for the highest competency in life in the discharge of his calling under God.

---

1. William Barclay, *Train up a Child: Educational Ideals in the Ancient World* (Philadelphia, PA: Westminster Press, 1959), p. 48.

2. ibid., p. 159.

Chapter 2

STUDENT PROBLEMS

IF WE BEGIN with false premises, we will consistently misunderstand and falsify every problem we face. Instead of solving our problems, we will aggravate them. The state schools are increasingly incompetent in dealing with problems of delinquent behavior, because they begin with false premises. As a result, they fail to grasp the nature of the problem which confronts them.

At the end of the 1960s, the Committee on Violence of the Department of Psychiatry, Stanford University School of Medicine, studied the problem of violence in the modern world. Never once in their symposium on *Violence and the Struggle for Existence* did they consider sin as the root cause of violence. Instead, in evolutionary terms, they saw it as an aspect of man's struggle to adapt to and cope with his environment. In fact, they saw as a "significant" contributing factor to social violence all restrictions on and "punishment of extramarital intercourse." In other words, Christian moral standards promote violence![1]

Such opinions, tracing delinquency and violence to environmental or evolutionary factors, are commonplace. A professing Christian, a principal of a state school, tried to tell me that all delinquency was traced to either environment or to heredity. When I cited numerous examples that gave the lie to his thesis, including one of a girl, born into a most amazingly depraved family, who, though raped repeatedly by family members and visitors as a child and as a teenager, became a happy Christian woman and mother after her conversion, he declared that it was "illegitimate" to

---

1. Frederick W. Ilfeld Jr., M.D., "Environmental Theories of Violence," in David N. Daniels, M.D., Marshall F. Gilula, M.D., and Frank M. Ochberg, M.D., eds., *Violence and the Struggle for Existence* (Boston, MA: Little, Brown, 1970), p. 88.

introduce theology into social problems! If God's Word and power do not govern every area of life, then He is not God.

The root problem in all delinquency at whatever age is always sin. In any case of unrepentant sin, the Bible gives the church a clear-cut duty: *excommunication.*

> Know ye not that a little leaven leaveneth the whole lump? Purge out therefore the old leaven, that ye may be a new lump, as ye are unleavened (1 Cor. 5:6–7)

St. Paul is here describing the necessity under God to purge out the delinquents, *the sinners.* His words apply to every Christian institution, the school as well as the church. It was the custom of orthodox Judaism, now less practiced than before to follow this practice, which has deep roots in the Old Testament, in the family. The service of the dead was read for any apostate member, and, until he repented, he was, to all practical intent, regarded as dead.

All too many Christian schools limp badly because of their disobedience at this point to Scripture. By failing to cast out the unrepentant, they allow the corruption of the whole body of children. It is important, moreover, for us to recognize what repentance means in the Bible. The word in Greek is *metanoia*; it means a turnaround, a change of life, of direction, of thought, and behavior. Repentance in the Bible is not a matter of merely saying, "I repent," or, "I'm sorry," but means a total change of life, from sin and ungodliness to faith and righteousness.[2]

The instruction in a Christian school is in terms of that life of faith and righteousness and service to God by means of that knowledge. There is a legitimate place for unbeliever's children in a Christian school, but there is no place for a delinquent child, no matter whose home he comes from. In some instances, the sinning child comes from the home of a church officer, pastor, and sometimes even a Christian school teacher. In any and every case, the integrity of the school requires a firm handling of the problem, and, if necessary, expulsion.

The most common excuse given by parents is that somehow it is the teacher's fault, and that, "The teacher doesn't understand my child." Both

---

2. See William Douglas Chamberlain, *The Meaning of Repentance* (Philadelphia, PA: The Westminster Press, 1943).

these arguments must be dealt with firmly. *First,* no teacher is perfect, and hence no teacher is faultless in dealing with a child. This is beside the point. The pupil has a responsibility to be obedient and responsive in the classroom, irrespective of the teacher, and the parent has an obligation to require this of his or her child. *Second,* it is not the teacher's duty to "understand" the child but to *teach* the child. Very few if any of my teachers understood me, and sometimes it was painful. However, they all *taught* me, and I was the gainer.

Moreover, the parents need to be told, firmly but kindly, that there is a difference between *defending* their child and *helping* their child. A child is often best defended from sin by being chastened. We help our children most when we compel them to see that they must conform to God's standard, not the world to theirs. A school, the child, and parents all suffer when a child's sin is not dealt with scripturally. A young man with a very high IQ, born of two brilliant parents, is today living on a meager income which requires supplementing by a working wife. He flunked out of college. His parents, because of their prominence in Christian circles, and their wilful obstinacy in defending their son, were never willing to face the truth about their son, and almost no Christian school teacher dared do so. The one who did was not backed by the principal and pastor. The result is a wasted life, two bitter parents, and a number of years of misery for some teachers. In this case, the child's sin was compounded by the parents, the teachers, principal, and pastor. *All sinned* against the Lord, and against other children, whose learning was disrupted by a wilful child. *We sin if we do not confront sin as sin.* We sin if we excuse sin and call it such things as "hyperactivity." The sin of a child should not be an occasion for sin by the school staff.

The Lord does not bless us for our sins, but for our faithfulness. It was Adam's sin that led to man's fall and misery. Sin is still our basic problem. A Christian school must not be delinquent in dealing with the problem of sin.

The most common reasons for failure to deal with sin in students are, *first,* fear of financial loss. The financial loss can be real, but the question is one of priorities. Which is more important, the financial return, or the blessing of the Lord and the welfare of the school? In the long run, moreover, a school which tolerates sin will suffer financially.

Second, there is the fear of the parents, usually because they are people of note in the community. If we are *governed* by such a fear, then we will be governed by these people in the school. We will forfeit authority in the school to spoiled children and the parents they control.

Third, there is the fact of moral cowardice. Dealing with difficult problems *is* usually painful, but the consequences of moral cowardice are far more painful.

Sin is man's basic problem. We cannot escape dealing with it in ourselves, or in any area of life. The Christian school must always be prepared to cope with it.

Chapter 3

HUMANISM IN THE CLASSROOM

IN THE LATE summer of 1978, the U.S. Internal Revenue Service issued some regulations designed to control Christian schools; on December 5–9, 1978, hearings were held in Washington, D.C., to give those schools an opportunity to protest. In the intervening time, some of us sent forth the call for Christians to rally to the defense of the freedom of Christ's schools and people. The reaction to this call in many areas of the church was to condemn those of us who issued it, to attack the Christian school again as a nonspiritual involvement in the world by Christ's flock, and to call for a "true" spirituality defined as limiting the jurisdiction of Christian faith to the church.

This is a serious matter. Under the surface, a vast area of hostility exists to the Christian school movement, both within the church and in the world. It would be easy to write at length about the many attacks on the movement: pastors who come to a church with a Christian school, who then work to close it down; congregations who scuttle a school when the pastor leaves, and so on.

It is important for us, very briefly, to cite the reasons for these attacks. *First,* many insist on limiting Christian concern to things which are spiritual. If this be true, then we must drop church weddings, and all concern over adultery and other sexual sins, because sex and marriage are declared by our Lord to be for this world only (Mark 12:25). All the same, Scripture legislates extensively and totally the sexual life of man. It also legislates concerning weights and measures, eating and drinking, debt, sanitation, and everything else. Very clearly, the Bible speaks concerning far more than our spiritual life. It governs our total life, because God is totally God, and there is no area of life and thought outside His government.

Psalm 139 tells us plainly that there is not a corner of the universe nor an atom of being outside of God's government. Hence, to limit the areas of Christian concern is to limit God and deny His Lordship.

Second, the Scripture is emphatic that our children must be reared in the Lord. This is a major stress of Deuteronomy and of Proverbs. Children are a heritage from the Lord (Ps. 127:3), and they must be brought up in the nurture and admonition of the Lord. In every religion, in varying degrees, the god claims the children. Molech worship and modern statism are classic examples of the claim among anti-God forces. We, however, must set apart our children for the Lord: they are His possession. This requires us to provide a Christian school.

But what constitutes a Christian education? Sometimes Christian schools are Christian in name only: they are humanistic schools with Bible added to a humanistic course of studies. It is a serious mistake to assume, *first*, of all, that there is any *neutral* subject which can be taught in the same way by both Christian schools and humanistic schools. To believe so is to deny God's total sovereignty over all things. It means that areas exist where man, not God, is the Lord. There is no area of neutrality in all of creation. What we believe determines our perspective in mathematics, history, biology, geology, art, physical education, and everything else. The triune God is totally the creator of all things and thus totally their Lord and determiner. All subjects are either taught from a Biblical, a theistic perspective, or they are taught from a humanistic, a man-centered perspective.

Second, we must remember that facts are never neutral, as Cornelius Van Til has so powerfully taught us. Before there is a fact, there is a faith. The faith interprets and determines the facts. The "facts" of the universe are very different for a Buddhist, an existential humanist, and an orthodox Christian. For the Buddhist, all is illusion and misery; his faith requires a world and life negation. *Maya* and *karma* determine all things. For an existential humanist, "facts" have only a purely personal meaning, the meaning which each man assigns them. Neither man nor creation have any essence, any created and preordained meaning. Good and evil and every other form of meaning is self-generated: they are values I assign to things in terms of my will. Nothing has any meaning from God's creative act; all meaning comes from man's creative act.

In Biblical thought, however, every fact is God-created and God-interpreted, so that the meaning of all creation is to be understood in terms of Him and His Kingdom. St. Paul makes it clear to the Corinthians that

> But with me it is a very small thing that I should be judged of you, or of man's judgment: yea, I judge not mine own self. For I know nothing by myself; yet am I not hereby justified: but he that judgeth me is the Lord. (1 Cor. 4:3–4)

The word Paul uses for *judge* is *anakrino*, to examine, investigate, and question. Paul simply says that he has no right to examine, inquire about, investigate, question, and judge *anything* in terms of his own standards and tests. Similarly, he has no regard for any and all such judgments made about himself. The only criterion for investigation and judgment is the Lord and His Word, and even then God's full and clear judgment will only be apparent plainly and totally with the Last Judgment (1 Cor. 4:5).

The plain implication, here and elsewhere, is that all study and investigation must be in terms of God's Word and the fact of God's sovereignty as Creator, Sustainer, and Lord.

Third, not only does faith determine facts, but faith determines the mind. The humanistic philosophy of education gives priority to the humanistic mind. Intellectualism is the determiner: it is the true morality. The greater the level of humanistic education, supposedly the greater the level of moral character will be. Salvation is thus seen as the spread of humanistic education and knowledge over all the face of the earth.

For us, however, the spread of humanistic education is the spread of sin and apostasy. For us, education is even more to be desired than for the humanists, but it must be godly education and in terms of God's whole counsel. Truth for us is not humanistic ideas, faiths and facts, but Jesus Christ (John 14:6), and for us "truth is in order to goodness," and also to true knowledge. A man cannot be holy or moral outside of Jesus Christ, nor can a man have true knowledge apart from Him.

This means that Christian textbooks are a necessity. We as Christians are members of another kingdom, the Kingdom of God. We live, not in a meaningless, blind, and evolving universe of chance, but in a universe totally created and governed by God the Lord. We dare not know anyone or anything apart from the Lord, because His Lordship, rule, and purpose are total. A school course which is not systematically Biblical is a hidden enemy to the faith. Humanism has no place in our hearts, churches, homes, or classrooms.

Chapter 4

THE TEACHER AS STUDENT

THE BEST TEACHERS are not Ph.D.'s; too many Ph.D.'s see themselves as finished products, with no need to grow. In my own student days at the University of California at Berkeley, it was the rare faculty member who continued his studies after becoming a full professor. Many of the older men used lectures first prepared about the time of World War I, told old and dated jokes, and were only vaguely familiar with the most recent research in their field. They had ceased to be students and were therefore irrelevant.

It can be objected that the university or college professor needs to grow, whereas a grade school teacher does not. What need is there for a first- or second- grade teacher to "keep up" with things and to grow as a student?

Learning involves, among other things, discipline, a desire to learn, and communication. We cannot give others a desire to learn if we do not have it. Most good teachers enjoy studying. A teacher can teach pupils *how* to read, but a *love* of reading comes in part from a teacher who shares it. As one who has always enjoyed history, I can recall the great variations in my teachers from grade school through the university in the teaching thereof. With some it was "deadly dull"; with others, it was an exciting unfolding of meaning.

Moreover, the greater our command of a subject, normally the greater is our interest in it. At the annual banquet of a medical society, I was amazed to find that the three doctors' wives at my table knew more about sports than most men, by far. They could cite statistics, recall plays, and give backgrounds almost like professional reporters. All had been originally totally bored by sports. On marrying doctors who had many evening emergencies, they turned to television, gradually became interested

130

in sports, and soon became remarkably well-versed in several sports. As their knowledge grew, their interest grew. Similarly, these three women had a very extensive knowledge in their husbands' areas of specialization in medicine and were interested in new ideas in their fields.

The teacher who does not grow in his knowledge of his subject, in methodology and content, is a very limited teacher, and his pupils are "underprivileged" learners.

Learning is in part a discipline. An undisciplined teacher is a poor learner and a poor teacher usually. What are the marks of an undisciplined person? The undisciplined person, whether a teacher, pastor, housewife, or businessman, has, *first*, a growing backlog of work which never gets done. True, many of us have work thrust upon us which is beyond our capacity to do in the time allotted to us, but, with the undisciplined person, necessary tasks remain undone.

Second, the undisciplined person finds his duties an unpleasant task because he is increasingly beset with a nagging sense of guilt because of all the unfinished duties. This sense of guilt leads to anxiety; it also pollutes one's rest, so that a vacation can be taken, but *rest* still escapes him. Life is thus clouded, and peace lost, because of unfinished tasks.

Third, an undisciplined person finds it difficult to get started with a task. The time is not right, or is too short, or he is too tired, and the work is postponed. If started, all kinds of little interruptions are engineered: sharpening pencils, getting a glass of water, and so on, supposedly to make work easier, but actually to kill time and postpone work. Thus, papers are not graded until the last minute; necessary reading is postponed, and so on and on.

How can we avoid this kind of problem? Or, better, how do we create it? Our problem is this: the work we least like to do, we postpone until last, and then, being tired, we have all kinds of "good" excuses for not doing it. The key to a work discipline is to do all those things we least like to do, or dislike doing, first. We do them then with a fresher mind. Having done them, we free ourselves to do those things we enjoy doing. Instead of working with a nagging sense of guilt, we work with a happy freedom. Moreover, we work with greater efficiency, effectiveness, and a clearer mind.

Another question in need of discussion is communication. In all teaching, we communicate with our pupils. One of the dangers in being a teacher or a preacher is that we are always talking. Talking can be a bar to learning and communication, or the most important means thereof. We can fill our speech with all kinds of extraneous data and lose the point. Some preachers talk on and on and never make a point. Others try to make their point with so many proof-texts and arguments that you finally forget what it was they were trying to prove!

Our teaching must be well organized and systematic; if we ourselves are not prone to being orderly in our thinking, our teaching will not be so. Thus, the superior teacher is always disciplining himself in order to pass on disciplined learning to his pupils.

The teacher as student is, above all else, a student of God's Word. To be a *student* means to advance and grow. A pastor whose children have all turned out badly has always had morning and evening Bible reading at the table. He thus reads Scripture constantly, at the table, at his study, and in meetings. However, he has no more insight into the meaning of any text in his preaching today than he had twenty-five years ago: he says the same things now that he said then, and without any growth in his knowledge of Scripture.

In brief, he reads as a ritual, and without understanding. We must also add that he reads without the Holy Spirit, for we are plainly told by our Lord that the Holy Spirit, above all else, is our teacher: "the Holy Ghost, whom the Father will send in my name, he shall teach you all things" (John 14:26). We are also told that the Holy Spirit is the foundation of all true learning: "But ye have an unction from the Holy One, and ye know all things" (1 John 2:20). Some of the other texts which speak of the Holy Spirit as teacher are:

> Howbeit when he, the Spirit of truth, is come, he will guide you into all truth: for he shall not speak of himself; but whatsoever he shall hear, that shall he speak: and he will shew you things to come. (John 16:13)

> But the anointing which ye have received of him abideth in you, and ye need not that any man teach you: but as the same anointing teacheth you all things, and is truth, and is no lie, and even as it hath taught you, ye shall abide in him. (1 John 2:27)

We are of God: he that knoweth God heareth us; he that is not of God heareth not us. Hereby know we the spirit of truth, and the spirit of error. (1 John 4:6)

The Holy Spirit is the teacher of "all truth." Only those who by the Spirit know Christ as Lord of their salvation can know Him as the Creator, and the Lord of all arts, sciences, and learning.

Our growth in teaching *requires* our growth through and under the teaching of the Holy Spirit. We must become good learners as a step towards becoming good teachers. Our profession is a very great one in Scripture: our Lord was a teacher, and the Holy Spirit is our continuing teacher. We cannot treat our calling lightly, nor grieve the Spirit by abusing our calling.

Chapter 5

SEXUAL DIFFERENCES IN THE CHRISTIAN SCHOOL

WE LIVE IN a humanistic era, and as a result the thinking of our age is dominated by humanistic ideas, so that both sides of an issue are commonly humanistic.

The word *equality* is a good example of this. It is a mathematical term, and it deals with abstractions. Thus, when we speak of equality *and* inequality, we are dealing with abstractions. Lumber, supplies, produce, and the like can be dealt with mathematically. But life is not an abstraction, nor are people, so that the introduction of the ideas of equality and inequality into human relations is illegitimate and only confuses issues.

In Scripture, the term *equal* has a very limited usage, and with the meaning of "no respect of persons." Because nothing a man is or does gives him any standing before God, in this respect all men are equal before God, equally reprobate outside of Christ, and equally elect in Christ.

Thus, as we come to problems of sex and race, we need to think Biblically. The Biblical emphasis is not a humanistic one. It does not place the emphasis on a standing among men, but on the calling and ordination of God. Not equality but differences are stressed, but not in any sense of conflict but complement. Dolen's comment is very good:

> First of all, what is sex? The word "sex" in English conies from a Latin word *secare* which means to cut or divide. And this usage probably originated from the Biblical rendition of the genesis of mankind. (Gen. 2:21ff.). In this account the first woman was made from the side of man. She was taken from him or divided from him. Science also tells us that there is a division or differences between males and females. The word "sex" indicates a division of mankind or a separation of mankind. There are elements or characteristics

that separate females from males. Sex has to do with these differences. Sex is difference, not likeness. Although males and females are alike in some ways (both have two arms), they are also unalike in some ways (genitals). The things in which they differ is the division between them.

Many times the male and female differences complement each other. Although there is a sexual division in mankind, each complements the other and both together make up something which should be regarded as a complete functional unit.[1]

Humanism denies both the difference and the complementary fact. The radical feminists are particularly extreme in their denial of the fact of differences. Humanistic education ignores the differences and has thereby contributed markedly to the disorientations of both men and women.

In ignoring and denying the differences, humanism is following its religious adherence to equality rather than any faithfulness to its own sciences. "Scientific" tests have indicated that there are racial and sexual differences. Standardized school tests are devised to avoid revealing these differences as far as possible.

The fact is, however, that intelligence and aptitude tests show that women surpass men in virtually every field, or at worst are as good as men, except two. The two areas in which alone men excel are aggression (Christians would say dominion) and abstract thought.[2]

This has implications for the classroom. Girls are usually the better students until advanced education begins, and abstract thinking, rather than concrete, becomes more important. There is another factor. Because girls are not concerned with dominion as are men, they are more ready to please a teacher and less independent of him in their attitudes. The girls become "teacher's pet," and the boys withdraw into a contempt for learning.

It is thus desirable, where the growth of a school permits it, to have separate classes for both boys and girls in each grade. It will increase the learning potential of the boys.

Reference has been made to racial differences. J. D. Unwin's study of

---

1. Walter R. Dolen, *Sex Makes the Difference: The Case Against Radical Women's Lib* (San Jose, CA: Walter R. Dolen, 1976), pp. 63–64.

2. Steven Goldberg, *The Inevitability of Patriarchy* (New York, NY: William Morrow, 1973), p. 209.

Sex and Culture (1934) made it clear that there is a mathematical correlation between sexual regulations and cultural achievement. Stated in Christian terms, his study means that, as men approximate or attain Biblical requirements for sexuality they also attain cultural, religious, and scientific levels of achievement. The lower the moral standards sexually, the lower the cultural level, until you reach the level of those who cannot count beyond ten.

Again we are reminded that it is necessary for us to think Biblically. The humanistic categories of equality and inequality should be alien to us. The key factors are grace, God's creation and ordination, and our faithfulness and obedience to Him. The Christian school must divorce itself from humanistic categories of thought.

This means, with respect to sexual differences, that they must be recognized as God-given and for the purposes of serving God's glory. We cannot view them humanistically. I have often pointed out that it is a great evil to speak of this as "a man's world." It is not a man's world, nor a woman's world. This is God's world, and we are His creatures, called to serve Him. Our differences are God-given and are to complement one another in His service and to His praise and glory.

Some current pseudo-evangelical thinking makes much of woman's duty to please, seduce, keep happy, and generally dance to her husband's tune. This is false. Man is not god; the Lord alone is God. Men and women are together to serve God, and the totality of their lives should be dedicated to pleasing God, not entertaining or pleasing the husband.

Dolen writes, concerning the biological weaknesses of men as compared to women,

> Males have greater quantities of biological defects than females: (a) more males are color blind; (b) more males are born stillborn; (c) male infants have higher rates of mortality and morbidity; (d) males are more susceptible to many diseases; (e) males grow and mature physically slower than females; (f) among males there are more learning and behavior disorders; (g) a higher percentage of males are mentally defective; and (h) males develop their verbal abilities later than females. These biological defects are felt by many to have something to do with males' XY chromosomes and other genetic and hormonal factors.[3]

---

3. Dolen, *Sex*, p. 66.

Perhaps we should add to this list the male illusion that God had no other purpose for woman than to please man.

For the Christian school to be truly God-centered, it must make both boys and girls look beyond themselves to the Lord. They must recognize that all their being must be given to the Lord and His glory, and that the differences in sex and aptitude are His ordination, and for His glory. St. Paul declares,

> For who maketh thee to differ from another? and what hast thou that thou didst not receive? now if thou didst receive it, why dost thou glory, as if thou hadst not received it? (1 Cor. 4:7)

The Christian school must do more than transmit information. It must communicate God's Word to the students in such a way that they see themselves, in mind, body, aptitudes, and sexuality, as God's creation for His glory.

Chapter 6

WHOSE CHILD?

A BASIC QUESTION which must be faced in order to give perspective to education is one of ownership. To whom does the child belong?

Statist educators have acted in terms of their answer to this question, and we will fail to grasp the implications of statist education if we miss their often plainly stated presupposition, namely, that the child is the property of the state. Harold Benjamin, formerly a professor of education and the director of International Educational Relations, U.S. Office of Education, 1945, was candid in his statement of the statist argument. We can, he held, come to grips with the problems in education by asking a few questions. One of these questions was this: "What Shall be Taught — and for What Purpose?" Benjamin, in his own way, wanted changed lives: "the end products in education should be human beings who have been substantially changed by their years of schooling."[1] The goal of education is "to make 'normal' persons" of the pupils, according to Lyman Bryson.[2] What constitutes a normal person, and what changes should be made in the child, the state and its education shall determine.

Van Cleve Morris tells us plainly that education, and every aspect thereof, must be either man-centered or God-centered. He then declares,

> If it is man-centered, then education should encourage the open and curious mind to inquire into and challenge any idea it chooses, trusting that "truth will out" in the end. If education, on the other hand, is essentially God-centered, then there will be certain subject matters which the child must learn of necessity and which lie beyond the reach of question and

---

1. Harold Benjamin, "The Problem of Education" in Lyman Bryson, ed., *An Outline of Man's Knowledge of the Modern World* (Garden City, NY: Nelson Doubleday, 1960), p. 383.
2. ibid., p. 374.

individual judgment. Since they are authored by God, not man, they do not have to be investigated or discussed, only learned in and for themselves . . .

You can readily see that here is a region where a great deal of educational dispute originates. For knowledge and truth are the "stock in trade" of the school. Where knowledge and truth come from, then, God or man, bears directly on how this basic "commodity" is retailed in the school.[3]

Morris's own faith in man is apparent from this statement. He ascribes an open mind and a trust in truth to the man-centered faith. In actual fact, all positions are more or less closed to other positions by their presuppositions. The man-centered faith has a closed mind where God is concerned. It believes that "truth will out" from man-centered sources, not from God. For Morris, the premises of humanism are naively assumed and never really questioned.

Morris does recognize "the ultimate moral nature of education,"[4] and he calls education "a moral enterprise."[5] His view of morality, however, is humanistic.

If humanism governs our perspective, we will answer the question, "To whom does the child belong?" in one of three ways. *First*, the older, individualistic humanism, while stressing the individual, was still respectful of the family. The child was thus seen as the property of the family. In ancient pagan humanism, as in Greece, Rome, and China, this was especially the case. Ancestor worship was a common expression of this form of humanism.

For us as Christians, the family is the basic institution in society, but the family is the trustee and steward of its children, not their owner. There is thus a vast and basic difference between the humanistic and Biblical views of the family.

Second, the child can be viewed as the property of the state. This view is basic to the philosophies of statist education. It is especially pronounced in all forms of Marxism, national and international socialism alike. The child is a state resource, to be developed and used for the welfare of the state.

---

3. Van Cleve Morris, *Philosophy and the American School* (Boston, MA: Houghton Mifflin, 1961), pp. 17–18.

4. ibid., pp. 18–19.

5. ibid., pp. 285–289.

It was the development of this view of man, of child and adult as properties of the state, which led to the development of state control of education. We cannot understand the governing philosophies of statist education apart from this premise.

Third, there is the view, held by existentialists and anarchists, that the child is his own lord and owner and not under state or parents. This view was popularized in the 1960s by the hippy philosophy. It is influential currently and is behind attempts to legislate a child's bill of rights. The *Playboy* "philosophy" is also strongly behind this perspective.

All too often, conservatives defend the first view, as though it represents a valid alternative. The fact is, however, that a Biblical faith requires us to declare that we are God's property (Ps. 100:3). Sheep are property, to be used as the Shepherd determines. We and our children are alike God's property.

Thus, our lives and our schooling cannot be for our pleasure or profit but for the glory of God.

What does this mean practically? *First*, it means that the focus of education is not on the child, nor on the parents, nor on society. It is on God. Education is thus primarily theological, God-centered, not vocation-centered nor knowledge-centered. Because of the Biblical doctrine of calling or vocation, the Christian school will strive to excel all others in preparing its pupils, but the focus will be on our necessary service to God. Because God's revelations give knowledge, and because knowledge is an aspect of God's image in us, we will seek to surpass all other schools in this respect also. Our focus, however will be on the competent and faithful service of God.

Second, worship and prayer will be a basic aspect of the school, because the students must never forget that all their schooling must serve not only themselves but primarily the Lord. In Psalm 119, we see the psalmist drawn ever closer to the praise of God by his study and his meditations thereon. Prayer and chapel in the Christian school should stress the absolute property rights of our Lord over us and our leaning.

Third, the school must seek to develop increasingly its freedom from and independence of state controls, state standards, and state accreditation. The root word in accreditation is *credo*, I believe. If the state is our

Lord, it is the state's approval and imprimatur we seek. If Christ is our Lord, it is the accreditation of His Word that we seek.

Increasingly, states are seeking controls over Christian schools and churches. They are demanding the right of lordship, accreditation, and licensure. This we must resist.

Chapter 7

BIBLICAL MOTIVATION FOR
TEACHERS AND STUDENTS

THE WORD *motivation* comes from the Latin *movere, motum*, to move. A motive or motivation is that which moves a man to action. From the Biblical perspective, motivation is both natural and educated. Thus, the motivation of the humanity of Adam, of fallen man, is the desire to be as god, to determine or know for oneself what is good and evil (Gen. 3:5). This motivation is natural to fallen man. Sin is basic to his being, i.e., lawlessness, "for sin is the transgression of the law," God's law (1 John 3:4). St. Paul is emphatic that, "There is none righteous, no, not one," "For all have sinned, and come short of the glory of God" (Rom. 3:10, 23). Sin comes naturally to fallen man.

On the other hand, the sophistication of sin requires education in sin. The unregenerate Australian native and unregenerate Russian or Chinese communist are alike sinners, but the sin of the communist is more deadly, because its motivation is not only a natural love of evil, but an educated one as well. Education enhances the scope of both good and evil.

The Christian teacher and student alike have in Christ a new nature. As such, they have, despite the continuing effects of sin in this life, a natural motivation to righteousness. Like their Lord, their new nature cries out, "Lo, I come (in the volume of the book it is written of me,) to do thy will, O God" (Heb. 10:7). Thus, the Christian child has a motivation to serve and enjoy God by virtue of his new nature, but needs at the same time training and discipline in the life of faith and the knowledge thereof.

We can understand motivation better by citing the fourfold estate of man. *First*, in the estate of innocence, in Eden, man's motivation and will were wholly good, but with the possibility of sinning. In this estate, man was given a task, to till and keep the garden, to classify or name the animals, and to discover the best possible ways to live and function in the Garden of Eden.

Second, in the state of depravity, fallen man had and has a will which is wholly evil, and a motive which is to be his own god, knowing or determining good and evil for himself and in terms of his will. The growth of fallen man is in terms of evil.

Third, in the state of grace, redeemed man, while still capable of sin, has a righteousness imputed to him, and a new nature given or created in him, so that his essential motivation is to glorify God and to enjoy Him forever. To do so, he needs education and development in terms of Christ's Kingdom.

Fourth, in the state of glory, man is wholly good in will and motive, and is perfectly sanctified, so that the possibility of sin is removed from him.

The Christian school will be dealing with children who are either in the state of depravity or in the state of grace; it will have both within its classes. The teacher sows the seed of God's Word, not knowing whether the ground be stony or fertile (Matt. 13:1–9) in most cases. How shall the teacher view the pupils?

First of all, the work of regeneration is God's task, and it is only within His power. Those who are regenerate manifest that fact in conversion, i.e., in faith and repentance, and man can play a part in conversion. The school, however, is not a church; its task is teaching, not conversion, although the ministry of the school is most effectual towards that goal.

Second, in many or most cases, the teacher cannot ascertain with assurance whether or not a child is a covenant-keeper or covenant-breaker, whether in the state of grace or the state of depravity. Looking back on my own boyhood schoolmates, I find that some who were docile and well-behaved later showed a reprobate nature, while some who were chronically restless and troublesome, or impish, only grew in grace and faith. It is easy to confuse a hereditary disposition to energy with rebelliousness.

There is, however, a *third* factor. Behind acceptable behavior, behind a conformity to Biblical morality and norms, there are two factors, faith, and the forming of sound and strong habits. In colonial and early

America, because all schooling was rigorously Christian, deeply ingrained habits provided a tremendous brake on sin. In 1815, the average age of criminals was forty-five; in 1960, it was nineteen. Thus, even for those in the state of depravity, a firm and substantial body of habits and years of training provide a deposit of results which inhibit and limit the workings of depravity. St. Paul speaks of this in Romans 13:1–7:

> Let every soul be subject unto the higher powers. For there is no power but of God: the powers that be are ordained of God. Whosoever therefore resisteth the power, resisteth the ordinance of God: and they that resist shall receive to themselves damnation. For rulers are not a terror to good works, but to the evil. Wilt thou then not be afraid of the power? do that which is good, and thou shalt have praise of the same: For he is the minister of God to thee for good. But if thou do that which is evil, be afraid; for he beareth not the sword in vain: for he is the minister of God, a revenger to execute wrath upon him that doeth evil. Wherefore ye must needs be subject, not only for wrath, but also for conscience sake. For this cause pay ye tribute also: for they are God's ministers, attending continually upon this very thing. Render therefore to all their dues: tribute to whom tribute is due; custom to whom custom; fear to whom fear; honour to whom honour.

Usually, the meaning of this text is limited to civil authorities, to whom it clearly does apply, and only too seldom is it noted that the text has a broader application, as verse 7 indicates. Even more, verse 1 is general: it is "the higher powers" who are to be obeyed. This obedience, of course, is always limited by our prior obedience to the Lord. No earthly power can command an unconditional obedience from us: only the Lord can.

Paul thus refers to all "the powers that be." This includes teachers and parents. The broadness of reference is apparent in verse 3, where doing good brings forth praise, something civil authorities do not commonly give!

Paul's point is, that, beginning with civil authorities, but certainly in-clusive of all the powers that be, God-ordained *and* faithful authorities will be a terror to evil works and the praise of good works.

In our day, this has been reversed. Sin is not seen as depravity but as deprivation. As a result, the powers that be seek to "make it up" to the sinner, to remedy the "lack" with love, special attention, and subsidies. As a result, such persons have created a market for evildoers: sin pays when it is viewed as deprivation, and the righteous are penalized.

The Christian school must restore God's requirements in order to get godly results. The sinners and the lazy need to be afraid, and the godly need to be encouraged and praised.

Some Christian schools seek to commend virtually every pupil for public relations purposes. In one school, first-graders received a large number of awards; almost every class member received one: for the best personality, most popular boy, most popular girl, and so on and on. There was one award for scholarship, and the second-best student was one of two students who received no award or certificate! Such a procedure is only evil and certainly not productive of sound motivation in the pupils.

Sound motivation is also important for teachers. Scripture says that the laborer is worthy of his hire, i.e., should be well paid (Luke 10:7; 1 Tim. 5:18). Newly established schools, and small schools, cannot always meet this requirement as well as they should, but it must be remembered that we cannot ask the teachers to subsidize the schoolchildren's parents by keeping tuition low, and therefore salaries low. This is a sin, and it is not blessed of the Lord.

In the educational process, the central motivating force, other than the grace and power of God, is the Word of God, which must be at the heart of the Christian school curriculum. Paul, in writing to Timothy, declares:

> But continue thou in the things which thou hast learned and hast been assured of, knowing of whom thou hast learned them; And that from a child thou hast known the holy scriptures, which are able to make thee wise unto salvation through faith which is in Christ Jesus. All scripture is given by inspiration of God, and is profitable for doctrine, for reproof, for correction, for instruction in righteousness: That the man of God may be perfect, thoroughly furnished unto all good works. (2 Tim. 3:14–17)

Paul gives us here an excellent statement concerning motivation in Christian education. *First*, the Bible alone can make us "wise unto salvation through faith which is in Christ Jesus." Moreover, "faith cometh by hearing, and hearing by the word of God" (Rom. 10:17). Timothy's schooling had been Bible-based.

Second, Scripture, being inspired of God, gives us the only sound doctrine, infallible reproof and correction, and instruction in God's righteousness or justice.

Third, the purpose of all this is "that the man of God may be perfect, thoroughly furnished unto all good works." All too many pastors and teachers assume that the goal of their work is to save souls for Jesus Christ. This is not the goal: it is the starting point of their calling. The goal is to train up those under our authority in God's Word so that they are well-fitted and thoroughly equipped for all good work, to go forth and to exercise dominion in the name of the Lord and for His Kingdom (Gen. 1:26–28; Josh. 1:1–9; Matt. 28:18–20). We are not saved just to be saved, but to serve the Lord. We are not the focus of salvation: the Lord's calling and Kingdom are. It is imperative, therefore, that the motivation of the Christian school be to train up dominion men and women. Education itself is a key to dominion, and hence the hostility of the humanists to the rise of the Christian school. The Lord says to us all, wherever we are, "seek ye first the kingdom of God, and his righteousness (or justice)" (Matt. 6:33), so that we are called to train up the King's men, His instruments for dominion, in order to bring every area of life and thought into captivity to Jesus Christ.

Chapter 8

THE PURPOSE OF LEARNING

IT IS A deadly error on the part of the Christian school to assume that its task is similar to that of the "public" or government schools with Bible added to it. There are no common sets of facts that are shared by both Christians and non-Christians. If we simply reproduce the same facts, we reproduce the same religion of humanism as that of the state schools.

But, some might object, can we not agree that Columbus "discovered" America in 1492? As a matter of fact, we must dissent with the whole interpretation of that event. For us as Christians, the facts are very different. Humanistic historians give us an economic motive, but Columbus had a very different goal. He was out to fulfil the prophecies of Isaiah; his eschatology was postmillennial. The gospel had to be carried to the far corners of the earth. He also believed that some "lost" tribes of Jews might dwell in the unknown lands, and he therefore took along an interpreter of Hebrew on his first voyage.[1] A Christian motive was present in virtually all the explorers, Pizarro being a notable exception. Louis B. Wright, in *God, Glory, and the Gospel* (1970), gives needed attention to this Christian motive in exploration, but none have yet studied its theological foundations. This Christian scholarship must do. The near coincidence of exploration and the Reformation is not an accident: both have a common theological source.

Facts and learning do not exist in a vacuum. There is always a context, and what that context is will depend on our religious faith and presuppositions. No fact exists in and of itself. When we ask the question, "What are the facts?" we are presupposing what the facts are that we seek. Thus, *the facts* of the physical universe differ widely for a humanist, a Christian, and a Hindu. For the humanists, all factuality is a product of chance evolution;

---

1. Simon Wiesenthal, *Sails of Hope* (New York, NY: Macmillan, 1973), p. 171ff.

all facts are thus ultimately meaningless, and their only reality is a physical one, and an irrational one. For the Christian, all factuality is God-created and the product of His eternal purpose; all facts are thus totally rational, because the mind of God is behind them, and their reality is thus more than physical and natural. For the traditional Hindu, all factuality is really illusion, because nothingness is ultimate; all things are burdened with karma, and their goal is release from the illusions of this world into final nothingness. What we call facts is determined by our faith.

What constitutes *learning* for us is also determined by our faith. Leonard tells us,

> *Learning itself is life's ultimate purpose.* This assumption has grave implications. If it is true, anyone who blocks learning, especially in a small child, is guilty of an enormous crime. The crimes against humanity, like the causes men are willing to fight and die for, do not appear all at once, absolute and sharply defined. Crimes and causes emerge gradually out of the clay of human experience.[2]

As a humanist, Leonard sees the subject matter of learning in humanistic terms.

Glock and Stark see the new source of divine revelation as science:

> There is a growing willingness to acknowledge that divine revelation is dynamic rather than static and that science may be the source of new revelations of divine purpose.[3]

They have no Christian conception of "divine revelation" in this statement. Their ideas come largely from Teilhard de Chardin's *The Phenomenon of Man* (1959). While they avoid commenting about the future of orthodox Christianity, their general tenor makes it clear that they see little place for it in man's future.

> The more fundamental question posed by the prospect of additional scientific knowledge about nature and about man is what its effect will be on the saliency of religion. If there is truth to the general theme we have been

---

2. George B. Leonard, *Education and Ecstasy* (New York, NY: Delacorte Press, 1968), p. 216.
3. Charles Y. Glock and Rodney Stark, *Religion and Society in Tension* (Chicago, IL: Rand, McNally, [1965] 1971), p. 290.

pursuing, there is the possibility that no one will care whether God exists or not because he will become irrelevant to everyday existence. If what can be attributed to God's will is made narrower and narrower, and if man's accountability for his actions is found to be more and more circumscribed, religion seems destined to lose much of its power to inform and guide the human condition.[4]

By "religion" the authors obviously mean Christianity; they themselves write as religious men, as devout humanists.

For such humanists, learning will be either for man's sake, or for society's sake. Leonard speaks of learning for learning's sake, but his view of learning is humanistic and a smorgasbord of individualistic and collectivist standards.

In any case, a humanistic view of education creates a set of facts alien to God's world and in conformity to man's goals. To illustrate, before the partition of India, Jawaharlal Nehru, in his world history, had no desire to offend Moslems. As a result, in writing about the massacre of Armenians by Turks in World War I and earlier, he actually said that the "truth" about the matter was that, probably, the Armenians massacred the Turks! This flagrant lie is of a kind common to modern historiography. Desmond Stewart, in *Life's* book on Turkey, refers to the massacres as a power struggle "between Turks and Armenians for the possession of Anatolian lands."[5]

For humanists, in other words, facts are what their personal predilections require them to be. Buchanan has called attention to this aspect of current reporting on Africa. A riot in South Africa is a front-page story about the horrors of South African racism. In Ethiopia, students are killed *en masse* by dynamiting, or by throat cutting, and most papers say nothing about this and other horrors in black Africa.[6] The Christian must condemn evil wherever it exists, *including himself,* because his yardstick is not man but God and His Word.

Everything that the state school teaches is governed by an overriding

4. ibid., p. 306.
5. See Desmond Stewart, *Turkey* (New York, NY: Time Inc., 1965), p. 29.
6. Patrick J. Buchanan, "Hypocritical Coverage," *Los Angeles Herald-Examiner* (July 4, 1977): p. A-10.

premise, *that man be served, not God.* Man can be interpreted collectively or individually, but, in any case, it is humanism.

For us, however, in the words of the Westminster Shorter Catechism, "Man's chief end is to glorify God and to enjoy Him forever." This must also be the goal of our education. We are called in Christ to be a royal and a priestly people (Rev. 1:6). This means exercising dominion in every area of life and thought under God. As prophets in Christ, we declare the meaning of God's Word for all of life. As priests, we bring all things to the Lord and dedicate them to the service of His Kingdom. As kings, we exercise authority and dominion in every sphere of thought and activity in the name of Christ our King.

The ungodly live and educate in terms of the great illusion propagated by the tempter, that man is his own god, able to determine for himself, in terms of his own man-made laws, what constitutes good and evil (Gen. 3:5). For us, there is no such problem: God's law-word is our standard, and the Lord alone is God. We educate in terms of this reality.

Thus, we cannot allow any element of humanistic education to govern our Christian schools. Humanistic schools belong to the world of Antichrist, and we to the world of Christ our Lord. We have different saviors, and different plans of salvation. We have also a very different kind of education.

Chapter 9

EDUCATION FOR FREEDOM

THE BASIC FORM of education is the liberal arts curriculum, i.e., the curriculum whose purpose is to further the art of being a free man. The problem, of course, is that there are differing definitions of what constitutes a free man. Even within humanism, there are variations of belief. In the Western world, we have the cynicism of Machiavelli concerning man, and hence the need for the control of most men by the superior few. We have Locke's passive, neutral man whose mind is a blank paper, and we also have the good, natural man, derived from one facet of Rousseau's thought.

Some humanists have summarized the issue as between the ideas of *man as pilot* and *man as robot*. In the *man as robot* view, most men need the planning and control of an elite group of men in order to achieve a "planned freedom." A Hebrew myth derived from Babylon, tells of another woman in Adam's life, the female-demon Lilith. Buford Stefflre cites this myth and asks, "Left to his own devices, will man woo Lilith or Eve?"[1]

These various forms of humanism all assume either a common goodness or neutrality in all men, or else a common evil which an elite group can escape. This evil thus is curable by man. The elite group can then control and direct all other men for their own welfare and gain a freedom for all men through the mediation of the elite philosopher-king or scientific, planning man. Freedom is thus a possibility for man through man and by natural means. The two basic instruments for the natural salvation of man

---

1. Buford Stefflre, ed., *Theories of Counseling* (New York, NY: McGraw-Hill, 1965) pp. 258–259; cited in Frank L. Field, *Freedom and Control in Education and Society* (New York, NY: Thomas Y. Crowell, 1970), p. 14.

are, *first*, education, and, *second*, state planning and control. Both these instruments are in full use today.

This salvation of man is not only to be attained by natural means, but it requires *freedom from God*, freedom from supernatural laws and standards, in order to secure *freedom for man*. To illustrate, the December 20, 1976 *New York* magazine suggests a reason why "musical superstar Leonard Bernstein" left his wife of twenty-five years, actress Felicia Montealegre. In commenting about some vocal sections speaking of death in Dimitri Shostakovich's Fourteenth Symphony, Bernstein said in part:

> Studying this work, I came to realize that, as death approaches, an artist must cast off everything that may be restraining him, and create in complete freedom. I decided that I had to do this for myself, to live the rest of my life as I want.[2]

This idea of living "the rest of my life as I want" is not limited to the artist. All humanists want this existential freedom, an independence from God, man, past, present, and future, to live out the demands of the ego, to be free to be one's own god, determining what is good and evil in terms of one's own desires. This is, of course, original sin as stated in Genesis 3:5; it is also existential freedom for modern man. Freedom from God means freedom from man also, because it is God's law which establishes man's duty to his Creator and to his neighbor.

In this point of view, education is self-realization, either as an individual or as a member of humanity. Freedom means, not salvation from sin through Jesus Christ, but the scientific method. It involves discarding all things which are not provable by the scientific method, and, of course, the scientific method for modern man presupposes that God cannot exist and that man's autonomous mind is the final arbiter of reality. In terms of this, freedom means the independence of man from God and from any God-given law and standard, so that law and morality are not God-given but are man-made and pragmatic and utilitarian. This educational goal of freedom is thus the freedom proposed by the tempter: "ye shall be as gods (every man his own god), knowing (that is, determining for yourself, in terms of what is best for you, what constitutes) good and evil (ideas which

---

2. "Lenny Faces Existential Truth," *New York*, December 20, 1976, p. 75.

are not absolutes but human constructs, in order for man better to realize his own self-created values and goals)" (Gen. 3:5). Freedom as defined by modern education is for Scripture simply sin.

Moreover, freedom in modern education means defiance, rebellion, and revolution. If man is free from any obligation to God, he certainly will feel no binding obligation to man. If God cannot command man, how can another man? Existentialism thus leads to a radical contempt for man, however much disguised. Humanism begins with the exaltation of all men as such and ends up as the exaltation by every man of himself and his own will. Quite logically, therefore, André Malraux once said, "I love to displease."[3] Malraux thereby established his existential freedom from man.

In education, this means a pupil who, as he grasps the meaning of humanistic education and its goal of freedom, is progressively in defiance of his parents, teachers, and society. Liberal and radical parents and teachers have quite logically applauded this defiance. For them, it is a most hopeful sign. It means that education is successful in part at least.

The goal of education, many hold, is to use Field's term, "a *personally meaningful* purpose system."[4] It cannot be an imposed purpose system from God; it must be "personally meaningful." To illustrate, modern art does not try to give us a structure in painting which has an objective meaning in God's world; a resemblance to that real world is coincidental, not basic. The painting may be blobs of color and random lines; the meaning is purely personal. The question is, what purely private and personal meaning does this painting evoke in me? In terms of that purely personal or contemporary evocation, what is art today can be a garbage-can reject tomorrow, or a relic for historians in a museum. Freedom in art means freedom from a given realm of reality and meaning in favor of a purely private one. As a result, art must seek the new and the novel to demonstrate its reality by a continuously fresh freedom from the patterns of the last hour.

Education finds it more difficult in curriculum to achieve a like contemporaneous freedom, but it cultivates this spirit more successfully than

---

3. "The Last Renaissance Figure," *Time*, December 6, 1976, p. 39.
4. Field, *Freedom*, p. 68. Italics in original.

the arts in the mind it creates. Whether in the arts, or with respect to tastes in music, dancing, or anything else, the student is a market for the new, for perpetual revolution against yesterday and today. This means perpetual revolution against himself, against what he is today in favor of some new idea of freedom. Not surprisingly, humanistic education produces not only a proliferation of sin, but of mental problems and serious personality disorders.

The contrast between the two goals of freedom in education appears dramatically in sex education. Humanistic education strongly advocates an "open" view, i.e., sexual freedom in the sense that the criterion in sexual behavior is man's desires and tastes. The intensity with which sex education is defended should not surprise us: it represents a very basic practice of the freedom to which all humanistic education points, the freedom for man to determine his own values and goals.

The Christian, however, also believes in sexual freedom, but he defines it differently. For him, sin is not freedom but slavery, and freedom is in Christ and from sin. For the true Christian, fornication, adultery, homosexuality, and all other forms of sexual sin are not freedom but repulsive forms of slavery. A godly marriage is for him freedom, because it is God's purpose and law; it alone gains God's blessing, and it alone gives him freedom under God in the sexual realm, unless his calling is to remain single. In any case, for the Christian there is no freedom except in obedience to God's law. He enters into freedom through the saving power of Christ; he lives in freedom by obedience to the law of God.

This means that Christian education emphasizes that freedom is through Christ's salvation and in obedience thereafter to the whole Word of God. Instead of teaching freedom as a radical independence from God, the Christian school teaches freedom as a radical and total dependence upon God. It insists on the interdependence of all men under God and in terms of God's law. It is thus a liberal arts curriculum for which Scripture is the key book, and in terms of which every subject and area is principled and informed. Teacher and student alike are under that binding word, and are free in terms of their faithfulness to it.

Both humanistic educators and Christian educators speak of furthering responsibility in their pupils. Humanism sees two kinds of responsibility. *First*, man can be viewed as responsible to society, to his country or to mankind as a whole. In this view, collective man replaces God as the agency to whom man is accountable. *Second*, man can be viewed as responsible to his existential self, called to rid himself of the accretions imposed by God, church, family, and society, and to realize himself as an existential man. Here, the individual replaces God. In both cases, freedom is from God to man.

For the Christian, man is responsible to God, and to man under God and according to the Word of God. Freedom is from sin, and therefore it is freedom from ourselves and from men, and from slavery and bondage to ourselves and to men, to become the covenant people of God in Christ, our Redeemer and King.

Christian education is thus not the curriculum with the Bible added to it, but a curriculum in which the Word of God governs and informs every subject. Only the Christian school, when it is faithful to Scripture, can have a truly liberal arts curriculum.

Chapter 10

EDUCATION & POWER

BECAUSE EDUCATION MEANS the training of the generations to come in the basic values, goals, and standards of a society, control of education is a central key to power. As a result, whereas previously education had been a Christian concern in the Western world, with the rise of humanism, in the form of the Enlightenment, education began to attract statist concern. The new church of modern man, its ark of salvation, is the state. Hence, modern man has progressively sought to bring education totally under the control of the state. In the various forms of socialism, national and international, this has been mandatory: education is made totally a state function, and neither parents nor the church are allowed a voice therein.

To control the future requires the control of education and of the child. Hence, for Christians to tolerate statist education, or to allow their children to be trained thereby, means to renounce power in society, to renounce their children, and to deny Christ's lordship over all of life.

How is this control to be achieved? To answer this question, it is necessary for us to examine briefly the premises of Auguste Comte, the founding father of sociology and a leading figure in the religion of humanism. For Comte, the history of man and his thinking has three basic eras or developments. The first is the era or stage of religion and myth. Man's search is for meaning, how to know and understand reality. Hence, he posits God as the great cause and as the source of meaning and the creator of reality. The second stage is philosophical and metaphysical. Man's quest is still geared to meaning and to understanding; it is still assumed that the universe is rational and has meaning, and the only problem is to understand it. The third stage is scientific and technological, or, better, methodological. Man now recognizes that meaning is a myth; the universe is not rational, and things are in essence meaningless. The reality is man. Man must renounce the quest for truth and meaning in any absolute sense and become pragmatic. He must use things and concern himself with methods of use, not the meaning of things. His instrument in this new perspective is science. Education therefore becomes anti-religious and anti-metaphysical. Instead of a study of the meaning of things, education becomes a training in the use of things in the service of man and the state. The concern of education is therefore not with truth and meaning, but with the pragmatic utilization of men and things to promote social welfare.

In this perspective, it follows logically that, meaning having been withdrawn from life and the universe, it is also withdrawn from man. Thus, according to Ross L. Finney,

> Physically we have become separate; mentally we remain but slightly differentiated participants in a common social plasm. Each person acquires a mind of his own only as he participates in the social mind. The notion of a separate and independent ego is an illusion.[1]

Man's individuality was for Finney "an illusion." Other humanists tell us that the state is an illusion, and only anarchistic man is real. Their nominalistic reductionism, however, leads to a universe of illusions, so that their very limited reality, whether the state or man, rests in an ocean of meaninglessness. Moreover, in terms of Comte, *meaning* is no longer a relevant category of thought: only *utility* is. Thus, whether the survivor in the humanistic universe is the state or man, both are there only to be used. Their only meaning is their utility. Man is thus a creature to be used; he has no meaning apart from that. The state, too, has no other meaning than its utility; it has no meaning in terms of God's order, the sinfulness of man, justice, or anything else.

Such a perspective leads to a radical externalism and superficiality. If the meaning is the use, and truth is not a valid category of thought, then education has a radically different purpose. It is no longer learning as understanding, but learning as a means of utilization and control. On

---

1. Cited from Ross L. Finney, *A Sociological Philosophy of Education* (1928), p. 145, by Erica Carle, *The Hate Factory* (Milwaukee, WI: Erica Carle Foundation, [1972] 1974), p. 22.

the university level, this meant the dethroning of theology and philosophy and their replacement by science and sociology. Traditional subjects had to be reworked into social sciences, sciences dealing with the planning and control of man. The goal of history teaching, once it becomes a social science, is to point to the need for a planned world order, and the past has meaning only insofar as it can serve as a prelude pointing to the world-state, the City of Man.

If the Bible has any place in the modern curriculum at any level, it is no longer as the Word of God; it is now taught as "The Bible as Literature," i.e., the Bible as a human resource for man's enjoyment.

This utilitarian, methodological form of education means that *externalism is now the means of salvation*. For example, a July 14, 1976, *Los Angeles Herald-Examiner* news story from Washington, D.C., is headlined, "Schools Bet on Cash to Stop Crime" (A-4). To combat crime in schools, both security measures and educational techniques are regarded as necessary, and "more money is seen as the ultimate weapon."

For this externalism as salvation methodology, the hope of man is in more social legislation, more money, more concentration of power into the hands of educators, politicians, and bureaucrats, and more controls over man and society. So cometh salvation!

But this is not all. Since externalism is now the means of salvation, it becomes an imperative to exclude Christians from power, because the Christian plan of salvation is a radical denial of this humanistic plan. Christian faith is centered on Jesus Christ, who declares, "I am . . . the truth"; He also declares, "I am the way," i.e., the method (John 14:16). Salvation is thus by truth, and truth is a person, the God-man Jesus Christ. From a world of meaninglessness and a utilitarian externalism, we are transferred to a world of total meaning, a world in which nothing is meaningless, because, "All things were made by him; and without him was not anything made that was made" (John 1:3). Moreover, according to Scripture, "Neither is there salvation in any other: for there is none other name under heaven given among men, whereby we must be saved" (Acts 4:12).

This means that power and salvation are transferred from man and the state to Jesus Christ, from the natural realm to the supernatural. For the Christian to come into power, i.e., to control education and the state, means the dismantling of all the key achievements of humanism and a radical denial of the humanistic plan of salvation. It means the scrapping of the modern humanistic power-state and its plan of salvation by law and education. It means the destruction of statist education and its humanism. It means moreover a change from methodology to meaning, from pragmatism to truth.

Education is thus the power area in the modern world and the arena for the struggle between Christianity and humanism. If humanism can retain control of the schools, the logic of education will then create more and more modernism, because modernism is simply humanism in charge of the church. It will turn evangelicals into neo-evangelicals and neo-fundamentalists. It will produce, in the supposedly Bible-believing churches, a faith having the form of godliness but lacking the power thereof (2 Tim. 3:5).

The recovery of the power of godliness requires a radical break, therefore, with humanism and humanistic education. It means that a thoroughly Biblical doctrine of education must govern the Christian school. Our hope, then, is not in externals and methods, but in that meaning and truth which is incarnate in Jesus Christ.

Chapter 11

THEOLOGY & PEDAGOGY

For a Christian philosophy of education, it is basic that teaching be founded on a sound theology and a Biblical doctrine of man. Christ being the Lord, man cannot be. The sovereignty of God precludes the sovereignty of man. The sovereignty of God means that our educational standards must be derived from Scripture, not man.

This means, *first*, that because Scripture makes it clear that man is a fallen creature living in a fallen world, education must deal with the fact of sin. Education is not evangelism: it is instruction. In every area of instruction, the presuppositions are drawn from Scripture, not from man. Thus, in biology, the basis for the theory of evolution is not in biological data but in man's attempt to eliminate God from the universe. The appeal of the theory is thus religious, not scientific; it explains nothing about the universe satisfactorily, but it does satisfy the humanist's hostility to God. A Christian philosophy of education will recognize the presuppositions of non-Christian education and concentrate on developing Biblical presuppositions as the only sound basis for a Christian perspective and answer. In other words, men think and act in terms of what they believe; faith governs life, and presuppositions determine our sciences, arts, and philosophy.

This means, *second*, as already indicated, that there is a necessary relationship between faith and knowledge. What we know is a product of what we believe. The growth of the sciences in the Christian West is not an accident. Only where faith exists in one God, whose counsel of predestination introduces total law and order into the universe, is science possible. Relativism makes science impossible finally, as does polytheism: no universe can then exist, only a multiverse which has no common truth or meaning.

Third, in teaching, it is therefore important to see the *unity* of man's being. He is totally God's creature, and he is a unity of faith and action. The Bible speaks of man's *heart* or *soul* as the center of his being, as the core of his conscience, consciousness, and thought. Out of it are the issues of life (Prov. 4:23), whether good or evil.

Paganism has held to a dualistic view of man, and sometimes a tripartite view. In Greek thought, man's mind and body were two different substances, and hence alien to one another. Virtue thus could be restricted to one sphere. Socrates could be regarded as a man of virtue while a homosexual. Conflict in man was made metaphysical rather than moral.

Because fundamentalism has a background of dualistic and tripartite views, it is readily antinomian. The doctrine of the "carnal Christian," a most pernicious view, holds that a man can be saved while showing no fruits of righteousness or of the Spirit. The spirit of paganism can be summed up in the common proverb, "You can't judge the heart." This presupposes that man's soul and body are two alien realms. Our Lord, however, makes it clear that a man is known and to be judged by his acts as a tree is by its fruits (Matt. 7:16–20). If we do not have a unified view of man, we readily fall into not only this "carnal Christian" doctrine, but antinomianism as well. It sees two plans of salvation in the Bible, a "progress" from the material to the spiritual, and from law to grace, whereas in Scripture salvation is always by grace, the "material" and "spiritual" alike created by God, both in the fall, and both redeemed, and grace and law both basic to God's being and plan, so that to receive grace is to delight in God's law.

Fourth, our perspective is to be determined by theology, not biology. Man is a product, not of biology, but of the creating word of God. This means that theological determination is prior to biology, and that a biological determinism is invalid.

Thus, the modern perspective sees adolescence and its storm and stress, its rebelliousness and spirit of independence, as biologically determined and natural to man. In fact, however, adolescence is a cultural product, a hallmark of a decadent culture, and almost unknown in the history of civilization outside the modern era. In most cultures, what we call adolescence is rather a time of the most careful and attentive imitation of adults and of the older generation. Youth, on the verge of mature life and work, is then most concerned about being closer to the adult world and accepted by it. Instead of rebelling against it, youth seeks admission and initiation into the world of adults. Only because existentialism places a premium on isolation and radical independence, do youth associate the dawn of physical maturity with a declaration of war and independence. They are simply enacting thereby the necessary religious "confirmation" rite of the modern world. The Christian child is confirmed in the faith of his fathers as he approaches maturity; the confirmation rite of the humanist child is adolescence and its rebelliousness or existentialism.

Similarly, Edward Shorter's research indicates that masturbation is a modern phenomenon in the main.[1] Masturbation is increasingly important in modern culture because it ties in with existentialist man's desire to be free of all other people, and thus to reduce sex to a purely existentialist act of one person, needing none other. As the existentialist temper of modern man wanes, so too will his emphasis on egocentric pleasures in any and every sphere.

Fifth, discipline is basic to Christian education, but discipline must not be confused with chastisement. The root in discipline is disciple, and true teaching makes the child a happy and eager disciple of Christ, ready to learn because it is a necessary and privileged aspect of covenant life that we be able and fully employed in God's service. Chastisement is a last resort, though a needed one. True discipline is positive; chastisement is negative. Discipline sets up guidelines, standards, requirements, tests, and measures. Discipline creates an inner clock and requirement, so that the life of the child becomes a progressively disciplined one, and the discipline becomes a natural part of the child's life, and permanently so. Discipline creates a living relationship between faith and habits, so that the person's faith is readily and fluently active.

Sixth, Christian education is of necessity not only theological in nature but theocentric. It is God-centered because God as Lord requires all things to serve Him. The Westminster Shorter Catechism tells us that "man's chief end is to glorify God and to enjoy Him forever." Every area

---

1. Edward Shorter, *The Making of the Modern Family* (New York, NY: Basic Books, 1975), pp. 76, 98–102, 106, 114–116, 251.

of life and thought must be in line with this purpose, and education especially so. Humanistic education seeks to glorify man and to enable man to enjoy himself; it is doomed always to fail. Christian education cannot be secular education plus the Bible. The Bible is not *added* to an existing curriculum; the Bible must establish, govern, and condition the curriculum, or else we do not have Christian education.

Chapter 12

THE IMPOSSIBILITY OF NEUTRALITY

ONE OF THE key myths of humanism is the idea of neutrality. It is held that the mind of man can be neutral with regard to facts and ideas, and that the scientific method is the way of neutrality. Man can, we are told, calmly and objectively approach and analyze facts and arrive at the truth.

Such a view presupposes neutrality *in the knower* and *the known*. With respect to the knower, man, it assumes that man is not a fallen creature, at war with his Maker. Rather, man is held to be a being capable of approaching factuality objectively and impartially, so that the basic judgments about the nature of things depend upon the mind of man.

For us as Christians, this view is false. If man is not fallen and dead in sins and trespasses, then man can save himself. Man's reason can lead him to Christ without the grace of God. Man, however, is fallen in all his being; he is totally at war with God. Fallen man may manifest no hostility to God, but his indifference is equally an act of war, because he has ruled out God from all consideration in all things. He has in effect declared that God is dead for him, and therefore need not even be considered or thought about. (If my children act as though I do not exist, nor am to be thought about, spoken about, or referred to, then they, without a word said, are manifesting hatred of me, and are warring against me.) Man is never neutral with respect to God, nor to anything that is of God. There is no neutrality in man.

Similarly, there is no neutrality in facts, in *the known*. The idea that facts are neutral is a product of humanistic and evolutionary thought, which holds that facts "just happened." They are ostensibly products of some cosmic accident and are thus uncommitted and meaningless facts. Hence, man can study them without any religious commitment; they are a neutral realm of being.

For us as Christians, however, all factuality is God-created, and hence the meaning of all things, including man, can *only* be understood in terms of the triune God and His Word. All things come from the hand of God, and we do not grasp the meaning of anything if we deny its Creator. The facts are *never* neutral, because they are God-created. Those who ask us to be "broad-minded" and approach the world and all factuality with an "open and neutral" mind are really asking us to presuppose a world which is the product of chance, not God. They are asking us to overlook the most critical factor of all, God, the Creator, and to presuppose that facts are a product of chance. Cornelius Van Til has pointed out that, "The war between Christ and Satan is a global war. It is carried on, first, *in* the hearts of men *for* the hearts of men."[1] This war is a total war. As Van Til so powerfully states it,

There is not a square inch of ground in heaven or on earth or under the earth in which there is peace between Christ and Satan. And what is all-important for us as we think of the Christian school is that, according to Christ, every man, woman, and child is every day and everywhere involved in this struggle. No one can stand back, refusing to become involved. He *is* involved from the day of his birth and even from before his birth. Jesus said: "He that is not with me is against me, and he that gathered not with me scattereth abroad." If you say that you are "not involved" you are in fact involved in Satan's side. If you say you are involved in the struggle between Christ and Satan in the area of the family and in the church, but not in the school, you are deceiving yourself. In that case you are not really fully involved in the family and in the church. You cannot expect to train intelligent well-informed soldiers of the cross of Christ unless the Christ is held up before them as the Lord of culture as well as the Lord of religion. It is of the *nature* of the conflict between Christ and Satan to be all-comprehensive.[2]

This total war is one which must be recognized, and education is at present perhaps the central theater of war. Van Til is right: "There are two, and only two, mutually exclusive philosophies of education."[3] These are Christian theistic and humanistic. Attempts to fuse the two are untenable (Matt. 6:24).

---

1. Van Til, *Essays on Christian Education*, p. 26.
2. ibid., pp. 27–28.
3. ibid., p. 36.

This means that the teacher cannot be neutral nor subscribe to humanistic philosophies with respect to his field of study. Either there is a neutral void behind every fact, or the living God. In our teaching, we will always consciously or unconsciously acknowledge one or the other.

In a neutral world, man stands as the sole voice of reason in a universal realm of irrationality. This makes man the high and ultimate judge and authority. The world is then under his interpretation and judgment, so that man stands over reality as its only lord and master.

Humanistic education fosters in its pupils the basic premises of Genesis 3:5. It asks man to be his own god, determining for himself what constitutes good and evil. Modern philosophers of education are often emphatic in declaring that there are no final answers. Hence their hostility to the Bible. To assume final answers means that there is a truth somewhere which stands apart from man and in judgment over man. To deny final answers and to affirm a perpetual quest, and a perpetual revision of all answers, is to affirm that it is not an answer or truth which is ultimate but *man*. As a result, modern humanism is hostile to the idea of answers. It prefers to speak of tentative answers and of paradigms which provide tools for using reality but never affirming any ultimate truth about reality. The ultimacy of man is thereby preserved.

This is the meaning of progressivism and instrumentalism. The Bible tells us that Jesus is the truth (John 1:17). Jesus makes the same statement about Himself: "I am . . . the truth" (John 14:6). Humanistic education denies that truth is a person or a thing. Experimentalism tells us that truth is what works for man.[4] With respect to truth, Morris holds that, "Taken literally, the statement 'I have found it' is not a scientific statement but more in the nature of a theological one."[5] Knowing is always a process, never a conclusion. *The truth is always contingent and relative to man.*[6] This, of course, is a theological statement, but Morris's god is man. *For us also truth is always contingent and relative, but to God, not man.* The existentialist also makes truth relative to man and his existential choice.

---

4. Van Cleve Morris, *Philosophy and the American School* (Boston, MA: Houghton Mifflin, 1961), pp. 155–165.

5. ibid., p. 159.

6. ibid., p. 164.

Truth is never abstract, nor is it some vague idea floating in the heavens. Truth is always relative to whatever is ultimate in our faith. If matter is ultimate for us, then truth is relative to matter: if mind, to mind. If man is ultimate, then truth is contingent and relative to man. For us, however, all things having been created by the sovereign and triune God, are relative to Him and to His Word. *Because* the Lord is the ultimate and sovereign Creator, He is therefore *the truth* in all its fulness, and all else is true in terms of its relation to Him. The more we understand the relation of the physical world in relation to God and His order and purpose in creation, the more we know the truth about creation. The logic of the humanist position requires him to say that truth is relative and contingent to man and his society because man is the ultimate truth.

St. Paul was aware of this element of humanism in the Greco-Roman world of his day, and hence his indictment of it as, "Ever learning, and never able to come to the knowledge of the truth" (2 Tim. 3:7). "Ever learning" is rendered by the Berkeley Version as "forever getting information."

Humanistic philosophies of education, and the state schools, are expressions of a religious faith, faith in man. Perkinson is right in speaking of "the Americans' faith in their schools."[7] Ours is another faith, and we must stand in terms of it, consistently and faithfully.

---

7. Henry J. Perkinson, *The Imperfect Panacea: American Faith in Education, 1865–1965* (New York, NY: Random House, 1968), p. 219.

Part V

Chapter 1

CHRISTIANITY VERSUS HUMANISM

THE GREAT ISSUE of the years ahead is the developing battle between Christianity and humanism. It is a war unto death. Christianity is a World and life view and faith, and it can only exist as such. It either is the Word of God for every area, or for none.

Christianity was born into the same battle. It is only the dereliction of Christendom which has led to a return to the beginnings of this old battle of the centuries. On the day of Pentecost, St. Peter's great proclamation was this: "Therefore let all the house of Israel know assuredly, that God hath made that same Jesus, whom ye have crucified, both Lord and Christ" (Acts 2:36). "Jesus is Lord!" This is the joyful and central proclamation of the early church. It is the declaration of St. Paul (Rom. 10:9; I Cor. 12:3; Phil. 2:9–11), and it is the joyful declaration that in Christ the prophecy of Isaiah 45:23 is fulfilled. To declare Jesus is Lord means that He is the world ruler who absolutely governs every sphere of life and thought. It is the obligation of every area to be Christian: church, state, school, family, the vocations, the arts and sciences, and all things else, must serve only Christ the Lord.

A problem in understanding the scope of our work is the common misuse of the word *church*. Our English word comes from *kyriakos*, a Greek adjective, as in *kyriakon doma*, or *kyriake oika*; our word *church* refers to an institution of worship, the ministry of the word, or a building. The New Testament word translated *church* is *ecclesia*, which gives the sense of two Hebrew words, *'edhah* (congregation) and *qahal* (assembly). It can refer to all the redeemed people, to their assembly in worship, their civil government, the family, the godly army, and more: it means the Kingdom of God. Thus, where Scripture speaks of the *church*, it means

Christ's realm in every area and sphere of life. All things must be brought under the dominion of Christ the Lord.

At present, humanism has brought all things, including most churches, under the sway of man the lord. The purpose of state schools, as laid down by Horace Mann, James G. Carter, and others, was twofold: *first*, to establish centralism, the priority of the state over every area of life, and, *second*, to eliminate Biblical faith. The founders of statist education in the United States were Unitarians. They rightly believed that control over the child through the schools is the key to controlling society. Control over the schools will determine control over state and church finally.

Christianity and humanism are diametrically opposed religions; one is the worship of the sovereign and triune God, the other is the worship of man. Let us briefly analyze some of the key points of difference between Christianity and humanism as they affect education. This is far from an exhaustive analysis. Our purpose is to provide a brief outline of some of the fundamental differences:

CHRISTIANITY	HUMANISM
1. The sovereignty of the triune God is the starting point, and this God speaks through His infallible Word.	1. The sovereignty of man and the state is the starting point, and it is the word of scientific, elite man which we must heed.
2. We must accept God as God. He is alone Lord.	2. Man is his own god, choosing or determining for himself what constitutes good and evil (Gen. 3:5).
3. God's Word and person is the Truth.	3. Truth is pragmatic and existential: it is what we find that works and is helpful to us.
4. Education is into God's truth in every realm.	4. Education is the self-realization and self-development of the child.

5. Education is discipline
under a body of truth.
This body of truth grows
with research and study,
but truth is objective
and God-given. We
begin by presupposing
God and His Word.

5. Education is freedom from
restraint and from any
idea of truth outside of us.
We are the standard, not
something outside of man.

6. Godly standards grade us.
We must measure up to
them. The teacher grades
the pupil.

6. The school and the world
must measure up to the
pupil's needs. The pupil
grades the teacher.

7. Man's will, and the child's
will, must be broken to
God's purpose. Man must
be remade, reborn by God's
grace.

7. Society must be broken and
remade to man's will, and
the child's will is sacred.

8. Man's problem is sin. Man
must be recreated by God.

8. Man's problem is society.
Society must be recreated
by man.

9. The family is God's basic
institution.

9. The family is obsolete. The
individual or the state is
basic.

The Christian school must thus teach every subject from a God-centered perspective, or else it will be teaching humanism. Mathematics, for example, has no validity in a universe of chance: it rests on the presupposition of a sovereign and predestinating God.[1]

The humanistic history book not only eliminates Biblical history and the great and central role of our Christian faith, but it sees history as

---

1. See Poythress, "Creation and Mathematics," *Journal of Christian Reconstruction*, vol. 1., no 1: pp 128–130; and Poythress, "Biblical View of Mathematics," *Foundations of Christian Scholarship*, pp. 159–188.

chance rather than purpose. History for the humanist is at its best simply man's determination, whereas for the Christian it is God's determination.

In the sciences, we must again deny the "rule" of chance. Materialistic determinism is no better. The Newtonian view of causality has collapsed because its single and purely naturalistic view is inadequate. There is no single cause in nature. Moreover, the multiplicity of causes does not suffice to account for the fact of order, design, and meaning. Only the presupposition of the God of Scripture can properly undergird science.

In literature, we must ask, what is a classic? The idea of what constitutes a classic has varied from culture to culture. Thus the great Vietnamese classic, *The Tale of Kieu*, is a masterpiece of humanism. It encourages self-pity, the indictment of God, and a belief that man, who has the root of goodness in him, is the victim of God.[2] A Christian classic must reflect a Christian world and life view; it must see conflict as moral, not metaphysical, and it must affirm an ultimate and basic harmony, not a conflict, of interests.

In teaching language, we must remember that grammar and culture are interrelated. There is a theological premise to grammar. Relativistic cultures cannot develop a truly future tense, nor a proper sense of the future. Words, moreover, represent meanings; they are miniature propositional truths. Communication is possible where a common culture prevails. The more existential that culture becomes, the more difficult communication becomes, because words and meanings are weakened or destroyed.

Christian faith is thus a total concern. Christian schools are a necessity, or else we will have anti-Christian schools. For Christianity to bypass education, to neglect Christian schools, is suicidal. Those who do so, have denied Christ and His lordship.

---

2. Nguyen Du and Huynh Sanh Thong, trans., *The Tale of Kieu* (New York, NY: Random House, 1973).

Chapter 2

HUMANISM:
THE ESTABLISHED RELIGION
OF STATE SCHOOL

JACQUES ELLUL, IN *The New Demons*, speaks of humanism as "an ideology that is unquestioningly adopted" by modern men who are hardly aware that there is any other position. It colors people's perspective and governs their minds as a kind of natural truth and law. "It is the basis for a vision of the world that all accept and for a common language and a norm by which behavior is judged." Ellul sums up the content of this attitude and faith thus: "First of all, man is the measure of all things." Second, "man is autonomous." Third, "man is a rational being." Fourth, man is free to choose between good and evil, and barring error, ignorance, and passions, he will choose the good. Fifth, "if evil exists . . . it is not the fault of man," but of "institutions, society, education, the economic system (capitalism), the division of society into classes, bureaucracy," and so on, but not man as such. Sixth, whatever is normal is good, and the normal is what the majority of our group accepts, which "means that in the last analysis everything can be permitted."[1]

Humanism is not only the current common faith, but, as Cremin admits, a millennial faith: man will bring in paradise on earth. Dewey in 1897 wrote that the teacher is always "the prophet of the true God, and the usherer in of the true kingdom of God."[2] Cremin shares this faith, and his purpose, like Dewey's, is to create the Great Community.[3]

---

1. Jacques Ellul, *The New Demons* (New York, NY: Seabury Press, [1973] 1975), pp. 26–28.
2. Lawrence A. Cremin, *Public Education* (New York, NY: Basic Books, 1976), pp. 76–77.
3. ibid., p. vii.

This should not surprise us. We cannot begin to understand the meaning of education and the function of schools, if we fail to realize, *first*, that *all education is religious*. Paul Tillich defined religion as ultimate concern. In education, our ultimate concern is the focal point of attention. Education in an Islamic society is thus different from education in a Christian society. There are different priorities. Each faith has its own basic philosophy of education. An educational philosophy common to all faiths is an impossibility, because the ideas of ultimate concern vary from religion to religion.

Second, the obvious fact is that all schools are religious establishments. For any civil government to enter into the financing and control of education means to establish a religion thereby. A century ago, the statist schools of America were an establishment, as Roman Catholics quickly recognized, of a semi-Unitarian Protestantism. The parochial-school movement was the result. At present, the state schools are an establishment of humanism. They teach and propagate a philosophy of life which does more than omit Christianity: it is radically at war with Biblical religion. Until we recognize that schools are establishments of religion, and that all education is inescapably a religious activity, we cannot come to grips with our cultural crisis. It is necessary, therefore, to recognize that the most central religious exercise of any culture is education. The religious faith of a society comes to focus in its education.

Thus Asahel Woodruff, in giving briefly his philosophy of education, has said:

> As has been said, creativity is often associated with rebellion, delinquency, and social disruption. Studies of creative people tend to support this notion by showing that creativity is associated with preference for change rather than stability; tendency to delay closure rather than to structure ideas; tendency to challenge old structures; tendency to let incoming perceptions dictate their own patterns, rather than to force preconceived patterns on them, and so on. Opposed to these tendencies are the overwhelmingly dominant tendencies of most people to maintain structure, and to find security in the maintenance of an unchanging environment. This tendency is deep-seated in the facts of human adjustment. It is perfectly natural, then, for most people to resent those who are unstructured and who are responsive to freshness and differentness because they are threats to security.

Dependence on external structure for security is a crippling condition. The democratic ideal (people thinking and making decisions) is its antithesis. It stands for a form of security which is derived not from external supports but from a sense of internal competence. I have seen beautiful examples of this kind of security in people who had lost all fear of change. The democratic ideal can never be attained until we transfer our base of security from external circumstances to confidence in the self. The first condition is a form of slavery. The second represents freedom.[4]

Woodruff is emphatically an existential humanist, opposed not only to Christianity but also to classical and idealistic forms of humanism. The kind of educational philosophy he represents is dominant today and very successful. By other standards, the schools of today are a failure; by Woodruff's, they are a success. We can regard the student "revolutionaries" of the 1960s, the sexual revolutionaries, and the hippies as failures, or as examples of freedom and liberation. Our philosophy of education will govern our evaluations.

Commager holds that America's schools not only manifest its religious faith, but that, "From the first . . . education was the American religion."[5] Garda W. Bowman and Gordon J. Klopf cite the question, "Should the school system be required to solve all the social problems of our time?" They answer:

To those who conducted demonstration training programs during the summer of 1966, the answer appeared to be that the essential criterion of any innovation in education is whether it helps to meet the learning and developmental needs of children and youth. However, they believed that the learning-teaching process can be truly effective only in relation to the totality of the child's social context, not in isolation.[6]

Horace Mann, in 1849, in his "Twelfth Annual Report of the Secretary of

---

4. Asahel Woodruff, cited in Robert C. Burkhart and Hugh M. Neil, *Identity and Teacher Learning* (Scranton, PA: International Textbook Co., 1968), p. xvii.

5. From Henry Steele Commager's *Living Ideas in America* (1951), pp. 546–548, included in Marjorie Mitchell Cann, ed., *An Introduction to Education: Selected Readings* (New York, NY: Thomas Y. Crowell, 1972), p. 153.

6. Garda W. Bowman and Gordon J. Klopf, from *Auxiliary School Personnel: Their Roles, Training, and Institutionalization* (1966), in ibid., p. 323.

the Board of Education," stated the religious calling of the state schools in words which Scripture applies to God:

> Without money and without price, it throws open its doors, and spreads the table of its bounty, for all the children of the State. Like the sun, it shines, not only upon the good, but upon the evil, that they may become good; and, like the rain, it descends, not only upon the just, but upon the unjust, that their injustice may depart from them and be known no more.[7]

Third, the function of state schools is thus a religious function. It seeks to promote and further a humanistic faith. The Ohio State Board of Education, in a "Statement of Philosophy," states plainly:

> The basic purpose of education is to perpetuate and improve the culture in which it exists. In our democracy the dignity and worth of the individual is of paramount importance, and each individual is expected to participate to the best of his ability. The mission of education in our country, therefore, is to provide for the fullest possible development of the talents and potentialities of our young people in order that they may participate effectively in the cultural, political, social, and economic life of our democracy. To accomplish this mission, an adequate program of education must be provided through our system of schools for all individuals regardless of race, creed, color or the economic conditions of the area in which they live.[8]

Culture, as Henry Van Til pointed out, is religion externalized: "a people's religion comes to expression in its culture, and Christians can be satisfied with nothing less than a Christian organization of society."[9] Similarly, the humanists can be satisfied with nothing less than a humanistic organization of society. A state-financed system of education is thus an establishment of some form of religion. The only escape from this is to establish none.

Ohio requires, according to its *Minimum Standards*,

> The board of education of each public school district and the corresponding body for each nontax school shall adopt a written statement of philosophy

------

7. Cited by Robert Ulich, *The Education of Nations* (1961), in ibid., p. 55.

8. John E. Brown, director, *1968 Minimum Standards for Ohio Junior High Schools* (Columbus, OH: State of Ohio Department of Education, 1968), p. 7.

9. Henry R. Van Til, *The Calvinistic Concept of Culture* (Nutley, NJ: Presbyterian & Reformed Publishing Co., 1959), p. 245.

and purposes for the elementary school or schools under their jurisdiction. Such statement shall have been developed through cooperative staff effort.[10]

The faith of the schools is expressed in its philosophy of education and in its curriculum. The basic curriculum of general education is very aptly called *the liberal arts curriculum*. We forget, through constant and casual usage, that this means literally *the art of being a free man*. The Ohio *Minimum Standards* consistently stress, not the Biblical standard of freedom, but an existential humanism. The emphasis is on experience and self-expression. Thus, for language arts, the philosophy statement stresses the importance of the subject for "the child's educational growth, social development, and future economic success." Moreover, we are told,

> Acquisition of language skills is fostered in a climate where children have the freedom, and encouragement and stimulation to express their thoughts verbally and in writing and to read widely.[11]

For an existential humanist, this is an excellent statement. For a Christian, there is no merit in freedom, expression, or communication *per se*. We are called by God to know, serve, and glorify Him, and language arts have this perspective. The original legal statement of the philosophy of education cited reading ability as basic to frustrating the work of Satan, the deluder, and was called the Old Deluder Act. The purpose of education was envisioned as *knowing God's truth*, not self-expression or communication as such. The two philosophies are a world apart.

The *Minimum Standards* give a philosophy of citizenship which is humanistic to the core: it stresses "learning experiences" towards fostering a humanistic community. The Christian's concept of community involves a principle of separation in terms of community in Christ, and of a mission towards all others.[12]

The philosophy of foreign language teaching is again humanism:

> Learning a foreign language at the elementary school level contributes significantly to the development of the pupil's potential talents and interests

---

10. Virginia M. Lloyd, *Minimum Standards*, standard EDb-401-02.
11. ibid., p. 31.
12. ibid., p. 30.

through broadening concepts of language and increasing the ability to communicate. It helps to create a better appreciation of life in other cultural and linguistic environments, enabling the learner to participate more effectively in a modern democratic society which maintains extensive political, economic, and cultural relationships with peoples of many languages and cultures.[13]

The focus here is again the individual and humanity, the family of man, not the family of God. Recalling again early American schooling, we need to remind ourselves that language teaching then had, at the elementary level, frequent instruction in Hebrew and New Testament Greek, in order to further a clearer knowledge of God's Word. The purpose of other languages at the academy level was to prepare those going into advanced studies to do their necessary research in the languages of scholarship. The function of such teaching was to arm God's potential servants with the best tools of the trade of scholarship. Such a purpose was pragmatic and theological. The present purpose, as in the *Minimum Standards,* is idealistic in terms of the family-of-man concept and anthropocentric.

The philosophy of social studies is particularly revelatory of humanism:

The term social studies designates that portion of the curriculum which deals with man in his relation to his social and physical environments. The social studies are concerned with how man is influenced by his environment; how he uses and modifies his environment to satisfy individual and group needs; how customs and institutions have emerged; how man is attempting to solve current problems; and how he draws upon his experience to plan for the future.[14]

The presuppositions here are evolutionary, not creationist. Man is a product of the natural environment; his "customs and institutions have emerged" from that environment; they were not ordained by God. It is not man's relation to God which is critical to our knowledge, but "his relation to his social and physical environments." "To plan for the future," man does not think in terms of the revealed Word of God but, "he draws upon his experience." The social sciences are in origin and theory a

13. ibid., p. 45.
14. ibid., p. 47.

humanistic and anti-Christian concept. Their basic thesis is the scientific prediction, planning, and control of man and society by man. The social sciences oppose God's predestination with predestination by statist man.

The philosophy of mathematics is also humanistic in the *Minimum Standards*. The critical question in mathematics today is this: is mathematics merely human logic, or is there a correlation between mathematical concepts and the factuality of the physical world? The Christian answer is emphatically *yes*, the humanistic answer of today is *no*. For the *Minimum Standards*, "the logical structure" is "of mathematics," *not of reality*.[15] Its view of mathematics is thus relativistic and existential.

The same lack of any belief in the reality of structure in the physical universe, a belief basic to Christian faith, because God is the creator, is apparent in the philosophy of science. The purpose of science teaching is, not to acquire basic information about the physical universe, but

> To acquire basic science information, including some fundamental concepts and principles of science.
>
> To learn to use the processes of study, investigation, exploration, and discovery used by scientists.
>
> To develop an appreciation of the attitude inherent in the scientific process.
>
> To apply the skills of inquiry to the solution of problems associated with daily experiences.[16]

Real knowledge about the physical universe is never mentioned, only knowledge about "science." The goal is not knowledge of physical reality, but "the solution of problems associated with daily experiences." This is a very clear expression of existentialism. It manifests plainly the surrender of the idea of a real world and objective truth which Gunther Stent, in *The Coming of the Golden Age: A View of the End of Progress* (1969), feels is contributing to the death of learning.

The philosophy statement concerning "Health" not only ignores the Biblical view of the body as God's creation, but assumes an evolutionary

---

15. ibid., p. 51.
16. ibid., p. 55.

situation of "changing moral standards and values."[17] For the Christian, it is not change or new values which are the problem but simply the old sin. Moreover, "successful social and family living"[18] is dependent upon one's relationship to God for the Christian, not primarily upon physical health and social judgment. To hold that "the health of the child is perhaps the greatest single factor in the development of a well-rounded personality,"[19] is to deny the primacy of faith and regeneration. The philosophy of "Physical Education" in the *Minimum Standards* is "child-centered."[20] This is logical humanism, but it is not Biblical faith.

The philosophy of the "Visual Arts" sees their purpose as "discovering and communicating his (man's) own humanity."[21] The Bible sees their function as God-centered, and "for glory and for beauty" (Exod. 28:40). The gap is between humanism and Christianity, and the one communicates man's glory, the other, God's. The same is true for music. The *Minimum Standards* see it as "an enriching force in the life of the individual."[22] The Bible sees music as a means of glorifying God, and man's enrichment in worshipping God.

For the "Applied Arts," the *Minimum Standards* have this to say:

Knowledge of today's technological society is essential to the development of the individual. His attitudes and outlook are directly related to his adjustments and responses to that society.[23]

Man is seen as a product of his environment, and his future depends on his "adjustments and responses" to society. We have throughout the *Minimum Standards* a different creator for man. For the Bible, it is the triune God; for the *Minimum Standards*, it is society and the state school. For the Bible, man's fall is from faith in God and obedience to His law; for the *Minimum Standards*, the fall is from the unity of the human community. For the Bible, salvation is through the atoning work of Jesus Christ,

17. ibid., p. 61.
18. ibid., pp. 60–61.
19. ibid., p. 61.
20. ibid., p. 64.
21. ibid., p. 68.
22. ibid., p. 74.
23. ibid., p. 77.

received by faith; for the *Minimum Standards*, salvation is by humanistic education and social action.

The *Minimum Standards*, *first* of all, establish a religious test for all schools, statist, parochial, private, and independent Christian schools. That religious test is humanism. *Second*, clearly there is an establishment of religion, and it is humanism, a nontheistic religion. *Third*, the distinction between state and non-state schools is disregarded and implicitly denied. The state legislates for the church and over the Christian and denies him freedom of religion.

Having said this, we must recognize that the *Minimum Standards* give us an intelligent and consistent humanism, missionary minded and zealous to conquer other realms.

The problem is that ostensible Christians are not as consistent as the Ohio State Department of Education, and other statist educators. Too often the churchmen halt between two opinions and have the power of neither.

Chapter 3

THE RELIGIOUS GOALS OF HUMANISM

THE CONCERN OF John Dewey with religion is too often overlooked, because Christians commonly identify religion with supernaturalism. Dewey himself criticized this identification.[1] With this, we must agree. Many religions are not supernaturalistic, and even fewer are theistic. Belief in God is not necessary to a religion, as witness Shintoism, Buddhism, Hinduism, Jainism, animism, humanism, and other faiths. Dewey regarded his position as a *religious* one. For him, truth came, not by revelation nor from the supernatural; rather, the "one sure road of access to truth" is "the road of patient, cooperative inquiry operating by means of observation, experiment, record and controlled reflection."[2] Dewey does not prove this: he assumes it; it is his basic religious faith and presupposition. He begins as a humanist. St. Anselm said, "I believe in order that I might understand." Cornelius Van Til has made it clear that all philosophies begin with a prior and religious faith. Dewey's faith is humanistic to the core. He is thus adverse to dogma and doctrine only when it is not humanistic. For him the "search for God" is invalid because it involves automatically a denial of his most fundamental faith, the trust in man's intelligence. In his own words, "Dependence upon an external power is the counterpart of surrender of human endeavor."[3] Such a quest for certainty from the supernatural is for him a denial of his fundamentalism, a faith in intelligence and natural means of inquiry.

But this is not all. For Dewey, as a humanist, the unity of mankind is an unquestioned and dogmatic faith. Anything which divides men

---

1. John Dewey, *A Common Faith*, p. 2ff.
2. ibid., p. 32.
3. ibid., p. 46.

between the saved and the lost, or divides reality with such terms as good and bad, true and false, is divisive. Dewey finds it impossible to ignore "the fact that historic Christianity has been committed to a separation of sheep and goats; the saved and the lost; the elect and the mass." For Dewey, this divisiveness is the ultimate sin:

> Spiritual aristocracy as well as *laissez faire* with respect to natural and human intervention, is deeply imbedded in its tradition . . . I cannot understand how any realization of the democratic ideal as a vital moral and spiritual ideal in human affairs is possible without surrender of the conception of the basic division to which supernatural Christianity is committed.[4]

The goal of history for Dewey is a humanistic New Jerusalem and millennial regime he calls, together with Graham Wallas and others, the "Great Community." There is *grace* in Dewey's religious world, but it comes, not from God, but from the human community:

> The things in civilization we most prize are not of ourselves. They exist by grace of the doings and sufferings of the continuous human community in which we are a link.[5]

Let us examine some of the implications of Dewey's faith as they appear in James Bryant Conant. Conant, a scientist, once head of Harvard's chemistry department, then for twenty years president of the university, chairman of the National Research Committee, high commissioner and later ambassador to the German Federal Republic, and a member of the General Advisory Commission to the Atomic Energy Commission, wrote several authoritative books on "public" education. In his autobiography he sees himself as a "social inventor" and subtitles it, "Memoirs of a Social Inventor." The term fits his role in education.

Conant often says that the Christian school has a right to exist, but everything else he says makes it clear that the existence of the Christian and private school is an evil. A "dual system of schools," for all his disclaimers of any attempt to suppress the independent schools, is for him the enemy of American society:

---

4. ibid., p. 84.
5. ibid., p. 87.

My book *Education in a Divided World*, published in 1948, was full of good words about American public schools. I had become convinced that the hostile and vocal critics were either misinformed or proponents of a dual system of schools.[6]

Let us examine a critical statement on Conant's study, one in which the implications of humanism for education and the family are openly stated:

Wherever the institution of the family is still a powerful force, as it is in this country, surely *inequality* of opportunity is automatically, and often unconsciously, a basic principle of the nation; the more favored parents endeavor to obtain even greater favors for their children. Therefore, when we Americans proclaim an adherence to the doctrine of equality of opportunity, we face the necessity for a perpetual compromise. Now it seems to me important to recognize both the inevitable conflict and the continuing nature of the compromise.[7]

The conflict is "inevitable." If a "retreat" is to be made, it is apparently not to be by the demand for equality. Since 1948, this demand has been stepped up, and educators have spoken of the necessity of separating at least the ghetto child from his family into campus boarding schools.

Conant spoke on April 7, 1952, on "Unity and Diversity in Secondary Education," before a meeting of the American Association of School Administrators in Boston, Massachusetts. As a defender of the true faith, humanism, he warned of the enemy at the gate, the Christian school:

But what I am more concerned with in the year 1952 is to make the hostile critics of the public schools in the United States show their colors. One of the most vocal of these is a Protestant clergyman who reveals himself when he writes, "The Communist is not, as a matter of fact, much of a revolutionist. The Communist would only substitute the logical secularism of Karl Marx for the pragmatic secularism of John Dewey." If this clergyman would start off all his attacks on modern education by stating that for him secularism and Communism are equal dangers, the reader would be in a better position to evaluate what he was about to read — or he might decide to skip it altogether.

There are many sincere Protestants, Jews and Catholics who believe that

---

6. James B. Conant, *My Several Lives: Memoirs of a Social Inventor* (New York, NY: Harper *&* Row, 1970), p. 613.

7. Conant, *Education in a Divided World*, p. 8.

secondary education divorced from a denominational religious core of instruction is bad education. They erroneously assume that the tax-supported schools are not concerned with moral and spiritual values.[8]

Like all humanists, Conant is given to misrepresenting the Christian position. We do *not* deny that the tax-supported schools are concerned with moral and spiritual values; we do insist that these humanistic values are anti-Christian and constitute an establishment of religion with the use of our tax funds.

It is worthy of note, that, when Conant gave this address, 92 percent of secondary-school pupils were in state schools; the number has declined since then as more and more Americans dissent with the established religion of state schools.

Conant saw a dual system of schools as something which "serves and helps to maintain group cleavages." This is true, but the Christian must answer that the alternative is a suppression of Christian training and ultimately of all religions save humanism. The *logical* humanism of Karl Marx holds to such a suppression; the *pragmatic* humanism of John Dewey accomplishes it only a step at a time, but it is no less committed to it. Conant affirms his faith in state schools as the means to true moral and spiritual values of a democratic nature. He says in part:

> By organizing our free schools on as comprehensive a basis as possible, we can continue to give our children an understanding of democracy by practicing it in school. Religious tolerances, mutual respect among vocational groups, belief in the rights of the individual are among the virtues that the best of our high schools now foster.[9]

For Conant's faith, Christianity is an optional and private concern; humanistic democracy is a necessary and catholic faith, to be taught to all and held by all. Conant granted "the rights of the individual," but *not* the rights of the group to their faith, nor of institutions such as Christian schools. He recognized the legal status pro tempore of the Christian school: he denied them a moral status as an evil. This is a part of a widespread trend in the modern world.

---

8. Conant, *My Several Lives*, p. 667.
9. ibid., p. 669.

The process has been and is one of *secularization* or desacralization—that is, the elimination of religion as a symbolic representation of social integration. In other words, religion per se is no longer the force that binds a society together. Instead, a modern society is held together by a mutual interdependence of the parts of that society including its institutions.[10]

This does not mean that the sacred is no longer with us. The modern state is divinizing itself. This was open and obvious with Stalin, Mao, Idi Amin, Nkruma, and others, but it is also true of all other states. We speak of national *shrines*; treason is now an offense, not against God, but against the state: it is the modern equivalent of apostasy. Our holy days are now national holidays, and the central power in society is not God but the state.

The god of society is the controlling force in a society. In the modern world, that power is the state. The God of Scripture controls man from within: the "coercion" is regeneration, a new birth, and it does not do violence to the person or his will. Statist coercion is external: it seeks to remake man by the total control of man's environment, mind, and education. The school is the key to statist coercion and control.

Thus, Field, in dealing with the psychopath in our schools and society, says that education "will have to employ powerful controls upon individual freedom in order to break existing antisocial 'sets,' habitual patterns, value systems, and the beliefs underlying them. The task will be to accomplish radical personal changes."[11] Some already classify the orthodox Christian as a social deviant or sociopath. In the Soviet Union, powerful controls are imposed on all such in slave labor camps, prisons, and mental institutions. The savage ridicule in state schools here of Christian faith is already a fact. Field wants reeducational centers, which he says will not be "full-blown concentration camps" because the prisoners can there "freely challenge the values society in general requires of them."[12] Such a challenge would be only a ticket to a longer term, we would have to answer. Field is so sure of the moral position of his own kind that he

---

10. Burton Wright II, John P. Weiss, and Charles M. Unkovic, *Perspectives: An Introduction to Sociology* (Hinsdale, IL: The Dryden Press, 1975), pp. 298–299.

11. Field, *Freedom and Control in Education and Society*, p. 45.

12. ibid., p. 46.

sees no comparison between his view and that of fascists and Marxists. Like all inquisitors, he is too sure of his righteousness to doubt that what he does is for man's best interest. Thus, he concludes,

> In summary, with regard to current educational needs, I am proposing: (1) that powerful control over individual behavior is not necessarily evil or anti-democratic; (2) that we already employ great controlling power in education; but (3) that we do so very ineffectively because we try to hide the fact even from ourselves; and finally (4) that when we clearly understand the need for power we will gradually require less of it, because its application will be overt, direct, timely, and hence necessarily more efficient.[13]

This is the democratic world of Orwell's *1984*. More accurately, it is the world depicted by Roland Huntford in *The New Totalitarians*.

The old totalitarianism, according to Huntford, applies physical coercion and torture to bring men under control. The new totalitarians use the schools and mind control. Sweden represents the new model totalitarian state, and its inspiration comes from American philosophies of education. The Swedish government hopes to introduce compulsory schooling at the age of three, because a commission of inquiry found that behavior is most easily influenced at that age.[14] Pupils are taught to reject traditional authorities in favor of the new, statist authorities.[15] The results in Sweden are similar to those of Israel's kibbutzes and the schools of the Soviet Union. Scientific research has declined, initiative is feared, "and the work is generally poor and unimaginative."[16] Prime Minister Olof Palme, in speaking to school children, said, "You don't go to school to achieve anything personally, but to learn how to function as members of a group."[17] Huntford comments, "To remain outside the group, is the sin against the Holy Ghost, and immense pains are taken to round up the independent and the unwilling."[18] Sweden has been de-Christianized even more than Russia.

---

13. ibid., p. 50.
14. Roland Huntford, *The New Totalitarians* (New York, NY: Stein and Day, 1972), p. 223–234.
15. ibid., p. 226.
16. ibid., p. 233.
17. ibid., p. 204.
18. ibid., p. 216.

The faith is seen as a form of mental illness.[19] The purpose of education is to serve the state and to promote economic efficiency.[20]

This is the new model for democracy: its great instrument of control is the state school. The struggle for Christian schools is the battle for the survival of Biblical faith. The Great Community of humanism is simply Babylon the Great of Scripture, the great enemy of the faith and of Christian man.

---

19. ibid., pp. 219–220.
20. ibid., p. 241.

GENERAL INDEX

A

absolutes, 13–14, 42, 48, 153
  and historiography, 41–42
  See also relativism
abstraction in academics, 74
academic freedom, 115–116
accreditation, 106, 140
A Common Faith (Dewey), 184
Adam
  and calling, 25
  and revolution, 22–23
adolescence, 161–162
American Indians and language, 49
anarchy, 7, 19, 97, 140
Ancyra, Council of, 108
Anselm, Saint, 16, 100, 184
anthropology and theology, 11
Apollinaire, Guillaume, 68
Aristotle, 5, 48
art, 182
  and relativism, 153
Atonement, the, and knowledge, 31–32
authority
  delegated by God, 144–145
  education and, 15–17
  See also sovereignty
autonomy and education, 17–18

B

Babel and communion, 96
Bach, Johann Sebastian, 81
Barrow, R. H., 5–6
belief. *See* faith
Bell, Charles G., 19

Benjamin, Harold, 138
Berlioz, Hector, 81
Bernstein, Leonard, 152
Blackmun, Harry, 105
Bohr, Niels, 69
Bowman, Garda W., 177
Bridenbaugh, Carl, 103
Bruno, Giordano, 72
Bryson, Lyman, 138
Buchanan, Patrick J., 149
Buddhism and reality, 127

C

capitalism, 41
"carnal Christian," 161
Carter, James G., 172
de Chardin, Teilhard, 148
chastisement
  sin and, 124
  vs. discipline, 119, 162
children
  anarchy and, 140
  ownership of, 138–141
  training of, 28, 119–121, 124, 127
China
  and education, 13
  and language, 49
"Chinafication of the West," 22
Christian curriculum
  abstraction and, 46
  academic freedom and, 116
  art and, 182
  civics and, 59–62
  dominion and, 27–29

ecology and, 10
economics and, 11, 14
focus of, 140
foreign language studies and, 13, 83–85, 180
foreign studies (general) and, 13
government and, 59–62
grammar and, 48–50, 51–52, 174
history and, 10–11, 42–43, 173–174
knowledge and, 26–33
language studies and, 48–50, 52–53, 174, 179–180
law and, 10, 14
literature and, 11, 14
logic and, 52–53
mathematics and, 13–14, 55–58, 173
music and, 79–82, 182
and need for textbooks, 128
not academic, 25
punctuation and, 51
science and, 11–12, 63–66, 67–70, 71–74, 75–78
Scripture and, 42, 47, 145–146, 154–155
sex education and, 154
student health and, 181–182
teaching Scripture, 44–47
writing and, 14, 48–50, 51–54
See also Christian Schools; education; curriculum
Christianity
  academic freedom and, 116
  citizenship and, 59
  civil government and, 103–107
  conflict and, 6–7, 12, 24, 105, 110
  contrasted with humanism, 171–174
  controversial vocations and, 108–110
  critical thought and, 24–25
  cultural retreat and, 29
  the "dark ages" and, 10–11, 40
  facts and, 147–148, 165
  foreign language studies and, 84–85
  investigation and, 128
  knowledge and, 166–167
  Manichaeanism and, 126
  progress and, 160
  reason and, 164
Christian parents and state schools, 110–111
Christian schools
  accreditation and, 105–106, 140–141
  assisting parents, 121
  and awarding pupils, 145
  civics and, 59–62
  discipline and, 120–121
  freedom and, 154
  gender difference and, 134–137
  importance of instruction, 45–46
  neutrality and, 60–61
  prayer and, 140
  purpose of, 32–33, 45, 61–62, 147
  regeneration and, 143
  sin and, 123–125
  success of, in 18th Century, 8
  teacher compensation and, 145
  teaching Scripture and, 44–47
  unrepentant pupils in, 123
  writing and, 51
  See also Christian curriculum; education; curriculum
church, the, 171–172
  capital crimes and, 108
  controversial vocations and, 108–110
  early church, 108–110
  Manichaeanism and, 112
  Neoplatonism and, 112
  origin of word for, 171
  self-discipline and, 120
  sins within, 108
citizenship, 59
civics, 59–62
Columbus, Christopher, 147
Commager, Henry Steele, 177
communion (sacrament), 96
community and communion, 96–98
  and crime, 97
  in early church, 109–110
composition. See writing
Comte, Auguste, 156, 157
Conant, James Bryant, 9, 185–188
conflict, 12, 24
  and Christianity, 6–7, 105
  with the world, 110
copying, to learn composition, 53
Cotton, John, 92
covenants, the, 95–98
creation, meaning of, 22–23
Cremin, Lawrence A., 175
criminals, age of, historically, 120, 144

critical thought, 15–25
  biblical Christianity and, 24–25
  humanistic view of, 24
  progress and, 21–22
  Satan and, 25
culture
  language and, 48–49
  mathematics and, 56–57
  religion and, 114
  stagnation of, 22–23
curriculum
  etymology of the word, 4
  liberal-arts, 4–6, 26–29, 151, 179
  non-Christian, destructive, 8
  and relevance to changing times, 13–14
  See also education; Christian curriculum;
    Christian schools

D

Darwinism and nature, 9
definitions and worldviews, 72–73
Dewey, John
  and democratic society, 9
  and pupil autonomy, 17
  on the purpose of the school
    environment, 21, 107
  and religion, 115, 184–185
  on the teacher as prophet, 175
  view of Christianity as divisive, 96
discipline, 119–121, 162
  in the army, 119
  regeneration, sanctification, and, 120
  students and, 122–125
  vs. chastisement, 119, 162
Dolen, Walter R., 134–135, 136–137
dominion, 106–107
  education and, 27–29, 101–102, 146
  power and, 33
  self-government and, 27
Dominion Mandate, 25
Dooyeweerd, Herman, 11, 16
Duchamp, Marcel, 53
Du Pont de Nemours, Pierre Samuel, 8

E

ecology, 10

economics, 11, 14
Eddington, Sir Arthur, 21
education
  18th Century, in the United States, 8
  absolutes and, 13, 14
  abstraction and, 46, 74
  authoritarian, 24
  authority and, 15–17
  autonomy and, 17
  change and, 99–102
  Christian education, 127, 155, 179
  citizenship and, 59
  communication and, 131–132
  communion and, 97–98
  controls and, 188–189
  critical thought and, 15–25
  cultural retreat and, 29
  curiosity and, 45
  as dedication, 28
  dominion and, 27–29, 102, 146
  evolutionary thinking and, 89–90
  existentialism, 20–21
  the Fall and, 89–94
  focus of, 140
  God's law and, 71
  Hebrew, 121
  the Holy Spirit and, 132–133
  humanism and, 4–12, 89–94
  humanistic goal of, 178
  in Rome, 5–7
  into life under God, 121
  knowledge and, 30–32
  knowledge of Scripture, 28–29
  law and, 7–11
  messianic role of, 23
  morality and, 114
  motivation and, 142–146
  obedience and, 25
  Pietism and, 12
  power, 156, 159
  Proverbs 22:6 and, 28
  purpose of, 3, 61–62
  relativism and, 97–98
  and relevance to changing times, 13, 14
  religion and, 3–12, 106, 176–183
  the resurrection and, 26–27
  Roman education, 121
  Scripture and, 44–47

Scripture central to, 145–146
theocentric, 162
tradition and, 121
welfare and, 106
See also Christian curriculum; Christian
    Schools; curriculum
Einstein, Albert, 69
Ellul, Jacques, 175
emotion, 80
enlightenment, nature of, 41
Enlightenment, the, 156
    Christianity and, 15–17
    humanism and, 8–9
    law and, 8–9
    social contract and, 95–96
environmentalist psychology, 107, 122
equality and truth, 134
escapism and music, 80
evangelism, 112
    and foreign language studies, 84–85
evil and human freedom, 68
Evolution theory, 63–64, 160
    and theory of education, 89–90
    effect on historiography, 41–43
existentialism, 153

F

facts
    interpretation of, 63
    meaning and, 98
    neutrality and, 32, 127–128, 147–148,
        164–167
    possibility for, 30
    See also meaning; neutrality
faith
    mind and, 128
    precedes education, 16
    understanding and, 100–101
Fall, the, 97
    and education, 89–94
family, the
    children and, 139
    humanism and, 9
    marriage and, 154
Field, Frank L., 153, 188–189
Finney, Ross L., 157
First Amendment, 103–105

foreign language studies, 13, 83–85
Foucault, Michel, 101
Fourteenth Amendment, 105
freedom, 151–155
    art and, 153
    evil and, 68
    lawlessness and, 68
    marriage and, 154
    science and, 67–70
    sin and, 153
    slavery and, 110
Freud, Sigmund, 91
Fritsch, Charles T., 28

G

Gay, Peter, 15, 16
genders, 134–137
Genet, Jean, 20
Gerard, R. W., 77
Ginsberg, Allen, 20
Glock, Charles Y., 148
God
    history and, 39–40
    personal control over creation, 69
God's law and education, 71
government, 59–62
    religion and, 104–105
grammar, 48–50, 51–52, 174
    absolutes and, 48
Gray, David, 11
Greek, importance of learning, 84
Greeks
    dualism and, 65–66
    education and, 4–5
    physical development among, 5
Greville, Fulke, 11
guilt, 90–92

H

Haeckel, Ernst, 74
Headley, John M., 39–40
health, of student, 181–182
Hebrew, importance of learning, 84, 85
historiography
    absolutes and, 42
    evolution and, 41–42

relativism and, 41–42
Scripture and, 42–43
a theological science, 42
twisting of facts and, 149
history
  Christian curriculum and, 10–11, 173
  God and, 39–40
  humanism and, 37–43, 173–174
  Scripture and, 43
  vs. social science, 37–43
Hoagland, Hudson, 78
Hodge, A. A., 92
Holy Spirit as teacher, 132–133
Hugh of St. Victor, 6
humanism
  applied arts and, 182–183
  art and, 182
  as state religion, 104–107, 114–115, 175–183
  autonomy and, 7
  Christianity and, 171–174
  community and, 96–97
  contrasted with Christianity, 172–173
  death of man and, 99–102
  education and, 4–12, 89–94
  facts and, 147–148, 149
  foreign language studies and, 83–84, 179–180
  freedom and, 151–155
  gender differences and, 135–137
  in education, 175–183
  in history, 37–43
  knowledge and, 30, 166–167
  language arts and, 179
  liberty and, 9
  mathematics and, 56–57, 77, 181
  music and, 80, 182
  religion goals of, 184–190
  responsibility and, 72
  salvation and, 128
  science and, 77–78, 181
  secularism and, 106
  sex education and, 154
  sin and, 122
  social studies and, 180–181
  student health and, 181–182
  truth and, 166–167
  unity and, 184–185
Hunebelle, Danielle, 55–56

Huntford, Roland, 189–190

I

Idi Amin, 188
infallibility and education, 23–24
Ingram, T. Robert, 28
investigation, criterion for, 128
irrationalism and evil, 68

J

Jackson, Jonathan, 111
Jaeger, Werner, 4
Jesus Christ
  as King, 32
  as Priest, 31
  as Prophet, 30–31
  is the criterion of light in history, 42
  sovereignty of, 171
  time and, 49–50
  truth and, 128–129
Jong, Erica, 90, 101
Julian (Roman emperor), 109

K

Kerouac, Jack, 20–21
Kerr, Clark, 115
Klopf, Gordon J., 177
knowledge, 26–33
  the atonement and, 31–32
  dominion and, 102
  education and, 30–31
  exhaustive vs. principled, 30–33
  faith and, 160
  growth in, 130–131
  and humanism's lack of answers, 30, 166–167
  must be organized in terms of God, 78
  science and, 181
  vs. wisdom, 44–45
Kuhn, Thomas, 58

L

language studies, 48–50, 51–54, 179

humanism and, 48, 179
impacted by Scripture, 85
Scripture and, 50
words and meaning, 51, 174
law, 104
central to Christian education, 10, 13, 14,
24–25
education and, 7–12
the Enlightenment and, 8–9
morality and, 114
learning, 130–131
Leonard, George B., 148
Levi-Strauss, Claude, 41–42
liberty, humanistic view of, 9
life, definition of, 72–73
literacy in America, 8
literature, 11, 14
autonomy and, 19, 20
definition of a "classic," 174
existentialism and, 20
Locke, John, 151
logic and composition, 52–53
Luther, Martin, 39

M

Machiavelli, Niccolò, 151
MacLeish, Archibald, 19
Malraux, André, 101, 153
mankind
chief end of, 162
development of, and humanism, 41–43
four estates of, 142–143
neutrality and, 164–167
purpose of, 146
unity of, 161
Mann, Horace, 8, 172, 177–178
Mao Zedong, 188
marriage and freedom, 154
Marxism
economic development and, 41
freedom and, 68
Marx, Karl, 41
Maskin, Meyer, 78
masturbation, 162
mathematics
chance and, 173
and correlation to nature, 99–100, 181

culture and, 56–57
humanistic view of, 56–57, 77, 181
in Christian curriculum, 13, 55–58, 173
neutrality and, 57
matter vs. mind, 65–66
Mauro, Philip, on Scripture as reliable
history, 42–43
meaning, 29, 63
salvation and, 158
Scripture and, 44–45
utility, 157–158
See also facts; neutrality
medieval Europe, 6–7
the "dark ages," 11, 40
mind
faith and, 128
vs. matter, 65–66
Moloch-worship, 110–111
monasticism and cultural retreat, 29
money, fiat, as theft, 60–61
Moore, Sir John, 19
morality
education and, 114
law and, 114
neutrality and, 60
relativism and, 91–92, 97–98
Morris, Van Cleve, 138–139, 166
motivation, 142–146
multiverse vs. universe, 115
music, 79–82, 182
emotion and, 80
escapism and, 80
evangelism and, 81–82
history of, 79–81
humanism and, 79–81, 80–81, 182
individualism and, 81
instruction and, 82
intellectualism and, 80–81
in the church, 81–82
purpose of, 82
the tithe and, 81
worship and, 81–82

N

naturalism, 68–70
Nehru, Jawaharlal, 149
neoplatonism, 65, 161

neutrality, 59–62, 127–128, 164–167
    the courts and, 105
    mathematics and, 57–58
    See also facts; meaning
Newton, Isaac, 72
Nietzsche, Friedrich, 91
1984 (Orwell), 189
Nkruma, Kwame, 188

O

Otto of Freising, 6

P

Palme, Olof, 189
Papy, Georges, 56–57
Petrarch, 40
Pietism, and education, 12
Pizarro, Francisco, 147
Plutarch, 49
poetry, 5, 11, 18–21
    anarchy and, 19
    existentialism and, 18–20
Polanyi, Michael, 58
polytheism, 115–116
postmillennialism and Puritan scientists, 72
Poythress, Vern S., 55, 57–58
presuppositions, 160
    Christian vs. non-Christian, 23, 32, 63, 71
    importance of, 11
psychology and theology, 11
public schools and crime, 97
pupils
    health of, 181–182
    rebellion and, 153
    soul condition of, 143
    unrepentant, 123
Puritan influence on science, 72
purpose, 27
    and life, 37–38, 107

R

reading, of Scripture, 46–47
reality, 69, 157
    education and, 25
    man's experience and, 25

science and, 65–66
    See also truth
rebellion and pupils, 153
Reformation, the, and law, 8
reform, path of, 110
regeneration as God's task, 143
relativism, 29, 97–98, 153
    and historiography, 41–42
    See also absolutes
religion
    and education, 3–12, 106, 176–183
Renaissance, the
    the "dark ages" and, 40
    government and, 7–8
repentance, 123
responsibility, 154–155
    humanism and, 71–72
    youth and, 161–162
resurrection, the, and education, 26–27
revolution, and Adam, 22–23
Rome
    conflict with Christianity, 105
    education and, 5–7
    law and, 10
Rosenstock-Huessy, Eugen, 21–22, 23
Rousseau, Jean-Jacques, 151
Ruffini, Remo J., 100

S

Salvadori, Mario G., 77
salvation, 158–159
    humanistic vs. Christian, 182–183
    meaning and, 158–159
    purpose of, 146
sanctification and progress, 23
Sarton, George, 75
Sartre, Jean-Paul, 91–92, 101
Satan, as the ape of God, 95
science, 63–66
    abstraction and, 74
    all is theological, 66
    chance and, 174
    the experimental method and, 75–78
    freedom and, 67–70
    humanism and, 77–79, 181
    impact of, 63–64
    the impossible and, 73–74

indefinable, 11
infallibility and, 75
knowledge and, 181
Neoplatonism and, 65–66
postmillennialism and, 72
reality and, 65
results and presuppositions, 77
teaching, 71–74
ultimacy and, 71–73
Scripture
child-training and, 28, 127
comprehensive, 126–127
education and, 145–146
exciting, 46–47
historiography and, 42–43
history and, 43
as history textbook, 42–43
humanistic view of, 46
impact on cultures, 85
inerrancy of, 47
infallibility of, 47, 146
meaning and, 44–45
as primary source of truth, 64
reading of, 46–47
teachers and, 132
teaching, 44–47
translation and language, 50
"secular," definition of, 106
Seidenberg, Roderick, 92
self-consciousness, 90–94
self-government, 27, 131
in American history, 8
sex education and humanism, 154
"sex," etymology of
etymology of, 134–135
Shelley, Percy Bysshe, 11
Shorter, Edward, 162
sin, 122–125, 142, 144–145
chastisement and, 124
Christian schools and, 123–125
confrontation and, 124
excommunication and, 108, 123
humanism and, 122
repentance and, 123
toleration and, 124
within the church, 108–109
slavery and freedom, 110
social sciences, 180–181

vs. history, 37–43
society and communion, 96–98
sovereignty, 6, 7–8, 15–16
accreditation and, 140–141
Moloch and, 110–111
of Jesus Christ, 171
presupposed for Christian education,
23–24, 160
See also authority
speaking, and composition, 53
Spengler, Oswald, 41, 56–57
Stalin, Josef, 188
Stark, Rodney, 148
state schools
and Christian parents, 110–113
as religious institutions, 176–183
state, the
and children, 139–140
and controls on education, 188–190
and divinity, 188
and establishment of religion, 103–106
and messianic role of education, 23
and Moloch, 110–111
and sovereignty, 140–141
humanistic nature of, 9
static nature of modern education, 13–14
Stefflre, Buford, 151
Stewart, Desmond, 149
stress and self-consciousness, 94
subjectivism and science, 21
Sunday-school instruction, weak nature
of, 46
Suppes, Patrick, 57
Swann, W. F. G., 76
Szczepski, Oleg, 107

T

teachers
as students, 130–133
communication and, 131–132
duty of, 123–124
neutrality and, 166
Scripture and, 132–133
self-discipline and, 131
teaching, 130–133
abstraction and, 74
importance of intellectual growth, 47

instruction and, 71
presuppositions and, 71
the Bible, 45–46
textbooks, necessity for Christian, 128
thought, 52
and writing, 53–54
Tillich, Paul, 3, 69, 176
time, 49–50
tithe, and music, 81
truth, 51, 75, 166–167
equality and, 9
and illumination by the Holy Spirit,
132–133
Jesus Christ and, 128
objective, 27, 116, 166–167
Scripture as primary source of, 64
See also reality

U

university, 102, 115
courses, 30
presuppositions and, 44
Unwin, J. D., 135–136
U.S. Constitution, 103
utilitarianism, 157–158

V

Van Til, Cornelius, 11, 184
and neutrality, 127
on Christ as King, 32
on Christ as Priest, 31–32
on Christ as Prophet, 30
on freedom, 68
on man's autonomy, 17
on man's goal of life, 93
on modern culture, 67
on neutrality, 165–166
on science vs. religion, 65
on Scripture and facts, 44
on the scientific method, 76
Van Til, Henry, on religion and culture, 178
vocations in the early church, 108–110
Voegelin, Eric, 41
Voltaire, 15

W

War of Independence, and establishments
of religion, 103
Webster, Noah, 60–61
Westminster Shorter Catechism
on Christ as King, 32
on Christ as Priest, 31–32
on Christ as Prophet, 30
on man's chief end, 150
White, John S., 7
Williams, Robert R., 109, 110
wisdom vs. knowledge, 44–45
Wolfe, Charles, 18–19
Woodruff, Asahel, 176–177
words, 51, 174
worldviews, and conflict, 12, 23
worship and music, 81–82
Wright, Louis B., 147
writing, 14, 48–50, 51–54
copying and, 53
existentialism and, 18–22
goal of, 54
logic and, 52–53
oral composition and, 53
thought and, 53–54
words, 51, 174

SCRIPTURE INDEX

Genesis 1:26–28 . . . . . . 61, 84, 107, 146
Genesis 2:7 73
Genesis 2:19–20 45
Genesis 3:1 25
Genesis 3:1–5 91
Genesis 3:5 . 25, 32, 78, 97, 142, 150, 152–153, 166
Genesis 22 111

Exodus 28:40 182

Leviticus 18:21 110
Leviticus 20:2 110

Deuteronomy (has verses on discipline) 120
Deuteronomy 6:7, 20–25 110
Deuteronomy 20:5 28

Joshua 1:1–9 146
Joshua 1:2–9 46

1 Kings 8:63 28

Psalm 30:4 82
Psalm 98:5 82
Psalm 100:3 140
Psalm 119 140
Psalm 127:3 127
Psalm 139 127

Proverbs (has verses on discipline) . . . 120
Proverbs 1:7 44
Proverbs 1:10 29
Proverbs 4:23 161
Proverbs 9:10 45

Proverbs 13:24 53
Proverbs 14:12 28
Proverbs 22:5 28
Proverbs 22:6 . . . . 28, 120
Proverbs 28:4, 9 53

Ecclesiastes 12:13 46

Isaiah 7:9 16
Isaiah 9:6–7 59
Isaiah 12:5 81
Isaiah 45:23 171

Jeremiah 31:31–34 112

Nahum 1:2–8 68–69

Matthew 6:24 165
Matthew 6:33 . . . . 61, 146
Matthew 7:16–20 161
Matthew 13:1–9 143
Matthew 19:26 73
Matthew 28:18–20 . . . . . .46, 61, 84, 146
Matthew 28:19–20 25

Mark 12:25 126

Luke 10:7 145

John 1:3 . . . . 31, 158
John 1:17 166
John 14:6 . . . . 128, 166
John 14:16 158
John 14:26 132
John 16:13 132

Acts 2:36 171
Acts 4:12 158
Acts 5:31 26
Acts 7:43 110
Acts 27 47

Romans 1:19–20 52
Romans 3:10, 23 142
Romans 4:24, 25 26
Romans 10:9 . . . . 112, 171
Romans 10:17 . . . . .45, 145
Romans 13:1 105
Romans 13:1–7 144
Romans 13:1–8 59
Romans 13:1–10 105

1 Corinthians 1:30 26
1 Corinthians 4:3–4 128
1 Corinthians 4:5 128
1 Corinthians 4:7 137
1 Corinthians 5:1–2 108
1 Corinthians 5:6–7 123
1 Corinthians 5:13 108
1 Corinthians 7:20–23 109
1 Corinthians 12:3 . . . . 112, 171

2 Corinthians 2:6–11 108

Ephesians 5:18–19 81
Ephesians 6:5–9 110

Philippians 2:9–11 171
Philippians 3:8 26
Philippians 3:9 26
Philippians 3:10 26
Philippians 4:22 109

Colossians 3:10 45
Colossians 3:16 . . . . 81, 82

1 Timothy 5:18 145

2 Timothy 2:15–16 45
2 Timothy 3:5 159
2 Timothy 3:7 167
2 Timothy 3:14–17 145–146

1 John 2:20 132

1 John 2:27 132
1 John 3:4 142
1 John 4:6 133

Hebrews 10:7 142
Hebrews 12:5–11 119

James 5:13 81

Revelation 1:6 150
Revelation 1:8 49

WORKS CITED INDEX

Italicized page numbers indicate that the material was quoted directly; non-italicized numbers indicate that the material was referenced, but not directly quoted.

1968 Minimum Standards for Ohio Junior High Schools (1968), *178*

1984 (Orwell, 1948), 189

"A Biblical View of Mathematics" (Poythress; in *The Foundations of Christian Scholarship*, 1976), *57–58*, 173

A Casebook on the Beat (Parkinson, ed., 1961), *20*

A Common Faith (Dewey, 1934), *9*, *96*, *115*, 184, *185*

The Age of the Earth and Chronology of the Bible (Rehwinkel, 1967), 43

A Guide to the Teachings of the Early Church Fathers (Williams, 1960), *109*

Anatomy of the Future (Seidenberg, 1961), *92*

The Ancient Engineers (De Camp, 1960), 40

A New Critique of Theoretical Thought (Dooyeweerd, 1953-1959), 16

An Introduction to Education: Selected Readings (Cann, ed., 1972), *177*

An Introduction to Systematic Theology (Van Til, 1976), *65*

An Outline of Man's Knowledge of the Modern World (Bryson, ed., 1960), 77, *78*, *138*

A Sociological Philosophy of Education (Finney, 1928), *157*

Auxiliary School Personnel: Their Roles, Training, and Institutionalization (Bowman, Klopf; in *An Introduction to Education: Selected Readings*, 1972), *177*

A World on the Wane (Levi-Strauss; Russell, trans., 1961), 42

The Banquet Years (Shattuck, 1961), *68*

Being and Nothingness (Sartre, 1956), *91–92*

Believing Bible Study (Hills, 1967), *25*

"The Brain, Mechanism of the Mind" (Gerard; in *An Outline of Man's Knowledge of the Modern World*, 1960), 77

"The Burial of Sir John Moore at Corunna" (Wolfe, 1817), *18–19*

The Calvinistic Concept of Culture (Van Til, 1959), *178*

The Christian Future: Or the Modern Mind Outrun (Rosenstock-Huessy, 1946), 22

The Civilization of Rome (Grimal, 1963), *5*

The Coming of the Golden Age: A View of the End of Progress (Stent, 1969), 29, 181

The Concise Treasury of Great Poems (Untermeyer, ed., 1953), *19*

The Constitution of the United States, 104

"Creation and Mathematics; or, What Does God Have to Do With Numbers?" (Poythress;

in *Journal of Christian Reconstruction*, Summer 1974), 55, 173
The Decline of the West (Spengler, 1944), *56*
The Defense of the Faith (Van Til, 1955), *30, 31, 32*
The Didascalion of Hugh of St. Victor (Taylor, ed., 1961), 6
The Dilemma of Education (Van Til, 1954), *17, 23, 25, 93–94*
Education and Ecstasy (Leonard, 1968), *148*
Education in a Divided World: The Function of the Public School in Our Unique Society
  (Conant, 1948), *9, 186*
The Education of Nations (Ulich; 1961), *177–178*
"The Elements of Life" (Hoagland; in *An Outline of Man's Knowledge of the Modern World*,
  1960), *78*
Ellicott's Commentary on the Whole Bible (Ellicott, n.d.), *26*
"The End of the World" (MacLeish; in Untermeyer, ed., *The Concise Treasury of Great
  Poems*, 1953), *19*
The Enlightenment: An Interpretation, vol. 1: The Rise of Modern Paganism (Gay, 1967), *15–16,
  16*, 40, 43
"Environmental Theories of Violence" (Ilfeld; in *Violence and the Struggle for Existence*,
  1970), 122
"The Environment Is Decisive" (Szczepski; in *Poland*, July 1976), *107*
Essays on Christian Education (Van Til, 1974), *67, 76, 165*
Experience and Education (Dewey, 1938), *17, 21*
Fear of Flying (Jong, 1974), *90, 101*
The Foundations of Christian Scholarship (North, ed., 1976), 55, *57–58*
The Foundations of Social Order (Rushdoony, 1968), 51
Freedom and Control in Education and Society (Field, 1970), *151, 153, 188–189*
"From Le Havre" (Bell; in Humphries, ed., *New Poems*, 1953), *19*
Giordano Bruno and the Hermetic Tradition (Yates, 1969), 72
Glimpses of World History (Nehru, 1934), 149
God, Glory, and the Gospel (Wright, 1970), 147
The Greek Experience (Bowra, 1957), *4*
The Hate Factory (Carle, 1974), *157*
"Historical Origins" (Rothbard; in *The Twelve-Year Sentence*, 1974), 111
History of the United States (Webster, 1832), *60–61*
The Homeless Mind: Modernization and Consciousness (Berger, Berger, Kellner, 1973), 49
Horizon (Autumn 1969), 101
"Hypocritical Coverage" (Buchanan; in *Los Angeles Herald-Examiner*, July 1977), 149
Identity and Teacher Learning (Burkhart, Neil, 1968), *176–177*
The Imperfect Panacea: American Faith in Education, 1865–1965 (Perkinson, 1968), *167*
The Inevitability of Patriarchy (Goldberg, 1973), 135
In God We Trust (Newman, ed., 1974), *92*
Intellectual Digest (June 1973), *100*
The Interpretation of St. Paul's Epistles to the Galatians, to the Ephesians and to the Philippians
  (Lenski, 1961), *26*
The Interpreter's Bible (1955), *28*
"Introductory Essay" (Sarton; in *Science: Religion & Reality*, 1955), *75*
Journal of Christian Reconstruction (Summer 1974), 55
"The Last Renaissance Figure" (in *Time*, 1976), *153*
"Lenny Faces Existential Truth" (in New York, 1976), *152*

Literature Considered as Philosophy (Knight, 1962), 101

Living Ideas in America (Commager; in *An Introduction to Education: Selected Readings*, 1972), *177*

Los Angeles Herald-Examiner (July 14, 1976), *158*

Los Angeles Herald-Examiner (July 4, 1977), 149

Luther's View of Church History (Headly, 1963), *39–40*

The Making of the Modern Family (Shorter, 1975), 162

"Man's New Dialogue With Man" (Levi-Strauss; in *Time*, 1967), *41*

"Mathematics, the Language of Science" (Salvadori; in *An Outline of Man's Knowledge of the Modern World*), 77

The Meaning of Repentance (Chamberlain, 1943), 123

The Messianic Character of American Education (Rushdoony, 1963), 23, 111

"Michel Foucault" (McMullen; in *Horizon*, Autumn 1969), 101

Minimum Standards for Ohio Elementary Schools (Lloyd, ed., 1970), 79, 83, *178–179, 179–180,* *181, 182*

Mitre and Sceptre: Transatlantic Faiths, Ideas, Personalities, and Politics, 1989–1775 (Bridenbaugh, 1962), *103*

My Several Lives: Memoirs of a Social Inventor (Conant, 1970), 185, *186, 186–187*

The Mysterious Numbers of the Hebrew Kings (Thiele, 1965), 43

The Mythology of Science (Rushdoony, 1976), 73

National Education in the United States of America (Du Pont de Nemours, 1800), 8

The New Demons (Ellul, 1975), *175*

New Poems (Humphries, ed., 1953), *19*

The New Totalitarians (Huntford, 1972), *189–190*

New York (December 20, 1976), *152*

Noble Savages: Exposing the Worldview of Pornography and Their War Against Christian Civilization (Rushdoony, 2005) 91

The One and the Many (Rushdoony, 1971), 32

Origins of the Medieval World (Bark, 1958, 1960), 11, 40

Out of Revolution: Autobiography of Western Man (Rosenstock-Huessy, 1938), *22–23*

Paideia: The Ideals of Greek Culture (Jaeger, 1945), 4

Perspectives: An Introduction to Sociology (Wright, Weiss, Unkovic, 1975), *188*

"Philippians" (Barry; in *Ellicott's Commentary on the Whole Bible*, n.d.), *26*

Philosophy and the American School (Morris, 1961), *138–139, 166*

The Philosophy of Physical Science (Eddington, 1939), *21*

Poland (July 1976), *107*

Popular Lectures on Theological Themes (Hodge, 1887), *93*

"The Princeton Galaxy" (Ruffini; in *Intellectual Digest*, June 1973), *100*

"The Problem of Education" (Benjamin; in *An Outline of Man's Knowledge of the Modern World*, 1960), *138*

Proverbs: An Introduction and Commentary (Kidner, 1964), *28*

"Proverbs" (Fritsch; in *The Interpreter's Bible*, 1955), *28*

Public Education (Cremin, 1976), *175*

Realities (December 1963), *56*

Religion and Society in Tension (Glock, Stark, 1971), *148*

Religious Concerns in Contemporary Education (Phenix, 1959), *3*

Renaissance Cavalier (White, 1959), 7, 8

The Republic (Plato, ca. 380 B.C.), 5

The Romance of Bible Chronology (Anstey, 1913), *43*

Sails of Hope (Wiesenthal, 1973), *147*

"Schools Bet on Cash to Stop Crime (in *Los Angeles Herald-Examiner*, July 1976), *158*

Science Digest (June 1977), *74*

"The Science of Personality" (Maskin; in *An Outline of Man's Knowledge of the Modern World*, 1960, *78*

Science: Religion & Reality (Needham, ed., 1955), *75*

Sex and Culture (1934), *135*

Sex Makes the Difference: The Case Against Radical Women's Lib (Dolen, 1976), *134–135, 136*

Smithsonian Treasury of 20th-Century Science (True, ed., 1966), *76*

St. Anselm: Proslogium; Monologium; An Appendix in Behalf of the Fool by Gaunilon; and Cur Deus Homo (Anselm; Deane, trans., 1935), *16, 100*

Teacher's Manual to Accompany Bruun-Haines, The World Story (Haines, 1963), *38–39, 39*

Theories of Counseling (Stefflre, ed.; in *Freedom and Control in Education and Society*, 1970), *151*

The Phenomenon of Man (de Chardin, 1959), *148*

The Tale of Kieu (Nguyen Du; Huynh Sanh Thong, trans., 1973), *174*

Thoughts Upon the Political Situation of the United States (Jackson, 1788), *111*

Time (December 6, 1976), *153*

Train up a Child: Educational Ideals in the Ancient World (Barclay, 1959), *121*

Turkey (Stewart, 1965), *149*

"Turning the Tables on Arithmetic" (Hunebelle; in *Realities*, December 1963), *56*

"Twelfth Annual Report of the Secretary of the Board of Education" (Mann; in *The Education of Nations*, 1961), *177–178*

The Twelve-Year Sentence (Rickenbacker, ed., 1974), *111*

The Two Cities: A Chronicle of Universal History to the Year 1146 A.D. (Otto; Mierow, Evans, Knapp, eds., trans., 1928), *6*

Violence and the Struggle for Existence (Daniels, Gilula, Ochberg, eds., 1970), *122*

Westminster Shorter Catechism (1647), *82, 150, 162*

The Wonders of Bible Chrononology (Mauro, 1961), *42–43*

The Word of Flux (Rushdoony, 1975), *101*

The World Story (Bruun, Haines, 1963), *37–38*

"Yesterday, Today, and Tomorrow" (Swann; in *Smithsonian Treasury of 20th-Century Science*, 1966), *76*

ABOUT THE AUTHOR

ROUSAS JOHN RUSHDOONY (1916–2001) was a well-known American scholar, writer, and author of over thirty books. He held B.A. and M.A. degrees from the University of California and received his theological training at the Pacific School of Religion. An ordained minister, he worked as a missionary among Paiute and Shoshone Indians as well as a pastor to two California churches. He founded the Chalcedon Foundation, an educational organization devoted to research, publishing, and cogent communication of a distinctively Christian scholarship to the world-at-large. His writing in the *Chalcedon Report* and his numerous books spawned a generation of believers active in reconstructing the world to the glory of Jesus Christ. For the last twenty-six years of his life, he resided in Vallecito, California, where he engaged in research, lecturing, and assisting others in developing programs to put the Christian Faith into action.

THE MINISTRY OF CHALCEDON

CHALCEDON (KAL-SEE-DON) IS a Christian educational organization devoted exclusively to research, publishing, and cogent communication of a distinctly Christian scholarship to the world at large. It makes available a variety of services and programs, all geared to the needs of interested ministers, scholars, and laymen who understand the propositions that Jesus Christ speaks to the mind as well as the heart, and that His claims extend beyond the narrow confines of the various institutional churches. We exist in order to support the efforts of all orthodox denominations and churches. Chalcedon derives its name from the great ecclesiastical Council of Chalcedon (A.D. 451), which produced the crucial Christological definition: "Therefore, following the holy Fathers, we all with one accord teach men to acknowledge one and the same Son, our Lord Jesus Christ, at once complete in Godhead and complete in manhood, truly God and ruly man..." This formula directly challenges every false claim of divinity by any human institution: state, church, cult, school, or human assembly. Christ alone is both God and man, the unique link between heaven and earth. All human power is therefore derivative: Christ alone can announce that, "All power is given unto me in heaven and in earth" (Matt. 28:18). Historically, the Chalcedonian creed is therefore the foundation of Western liberty, for it sets limits on all authoritarian human institutions by acknowledging the validity of the claims of the One who is the source of true human freedom (Gal. 5:1). The Chalcedon Foundation publishes books under its own name and that of Ross House Books. It produces a magazine, *Faith for All of Life*, and a newsletter, the *Chalcedon Report*, both bimonthly. All gifts to Chalcedon are tax deductible. For a complimentary trial subscription, or information on other book titles, please contact:

Chalcedon • Box 158 • Vallecito, CA 95251 USA
www.chalcedon.edu

CPSIA information can be obtained
at www.ICGtesting.com
Printed in the USA
FSOW04n0448240316
18213FS